THE ORDER OF MASS

According to the Extraordinary Form of the Roman Rite: The Missal of Blessed John XXIII

prepared by
Michael Sternbeck

IGNATIUS PRESS   SAN FRANCISCO
MMVIII

Nihil obstat:

The Rev. G. E. Tattersall, *censor deputatus*

Imprimatur:

The Most Reverend Denis J. Hart,
Archbishop of Melbourne
24th August 2007

www.saintbedestudio.bizland.com

Translation of the Order of Mass (Missale Romanum 1962) and
Prefaces (Missale Romanum 1970)
Introduction, commentaries and typesetting
© Michael Sternbeck, 2008
Newcastle, Australia

Cover design by Michael Sternbeck

ISBN 978-1-58617-243-5
Library of Congress Control Number 2007942937

Printed in the United States of America ∞

On the use of this Mass-book

This Mass-book, in addition to being a complete text and translation of the Order of Mass according to the 1962 Missale Romanum, also features an introduction discussing the nature of the Mass and how it differs from the New Order of Mass; it also includes devotional prayers for use before and after Mass. It is not only meant for use at Mass: it is also designed to be read at home, so to allow everyone to participate as fully as possible through their knowledge of the nature of the Mass, its structure and its prayers. Alongside the Latin prayers of the Mass, a translation into modern English is given, together with a commentary on the origins and significance of many of the prayers. In the margin next to the Latin prayers, directions are given in **bold print** about when to stand, sit or kneel.

Many of the prayers of the 1962 Missale Romanum (unlike the New Order of Mass) are recited quietly and alone by the celebrant. Some prayers and invitations are responded to by the minister alone; these appear like this (e.g.):

C. Domine, exaudi orationem meam.	C. Lord, hear my prayer.
M. Et clamor meus ad te veniat.	M. And let my cry come to you.
C. Dominus vobiscum.	C. The Lord be with you.
to which the minister alone responds:	
Et cum spiritu tuo.	M. And with your spirit.

Other invitations, however, are responded to by all present; at a Low Masses these would be said, at a High Masses they would be sung; they appear like this in the Mass-book:

Celebrant: Dominus vobiscum.

ALL RESPOND: **Et cum spiritu tuo.**

Celebrant: Oremus.

Finally, this Mass-book is meant to be used with your own missal or a leaflet which contains the Proper of the Mass of the Day. In this booklet, the following words indicate when you need to turn to your Missal or the Mass sheet for a prayer or reading:

Proper of the Mass for the Day

This volume is dedicated to the memory of my devoted parents:

Kevin John Sternbeck (1920–1996)

Clare Jane Sternbeck (1922–2007)

Commentaries on the prayers and ceremonies of the Mass were prepared by Michael Sternbeck with the assistance of Father Glen Tattersall and with reference to the writings of August Croegaert (*The Mass: A Liturgical Commentary*, 2 vols. Burns and Oates, London, 1959); Francois Amiot (History of the Mass Guild Press, New York, 1958); Adrian Fortescue (*The Mass*, Longmans, London, 1912); Josef Jungmann (*The Early Liturgy*, Notre Dame Press, Indiana, 1959); Pius Parsch (*The Liturgy of the Mass*, Herder, London, 1957) Ludwig Eisenhofer and Joseph Lechner (*The Liturgy of the Roman Rite*, Herder, Freiburg, 1961), Hubert McEvoy SJ (*Priestly Prayers*, Burns and Oates, London, 1961), John Coventry SJ (*The Life Story of the Mass*, Harvill Press, London, 1960), William O'Shea SS (*The Worship of the Church*, Newman Press, Maryland, 1957) and Archdale King (*Liturgy of the Roman Church*, Bruce Publishing, 1957). The translations of the Canon of the Mass and the Last Gospel are adapted from a translation by Monsignor Ronald Knox, under licence from Burns and Oates.

CONTENTS

FOREWORD

James Goold House
P.O. Box 146
East Melbourne Vic 3002
Australia

From my youth I have valued and loved the traditional Mass of the Roman Rite. Since 1970, I have grown to love the Missal of Paul VI. I am delighted that the Missal of Blessed John XXIII has been restored as the Extraordinary form of Mass in the Roman Rite because of the spiritual values it contains, together with the focus on worship with Christ to the Father.

This Mass book invites us to be drawn into the mystery which is God's love for us in giving his own Son at the Last Supper and on Calvary for our redemption. The book will serve to help us understand the prayers and be united with the priest in offering the one, perfect, unbloody sacrifice to God the Father, which brought our redemption.

A careful use of the prayers of this Mass will lead us into deeper union with Christ as we realise our own unworthiness and need of forgiveness and rejoice with him in the loving initiative by which Jesus went to the Cross to save us.

I congratulate Michael Sternbeck on the work that he has done so carefully. The appearance of this book will be very timely as people once again become familiar with the traditional form of the Roman Rite in Latin. May this book be an instrument of holiness, peace, prayer and inspiration to all who use it.

+ Denis J. Hart

Feast of Saint Bartholomew, Apostle
24th August 2007

+ Denis J. Hart
ARCHBISHOP OF MELBOURNE

INTRODUCTION

The sacred nature of the Mass

"O sacred banquet in which Christ is received, in which the memory of his passion is recalled...and a pledge of future glory is given to us!" (Thomas Aquinas).

Our Lord Jesus Christ offered himself to God the Father once upon the Cross for our eternal redemption. But at the Last Supper, so that the commemoration of His Sacrifice might remain throughout all ages, Christ offered to the Father His own body and blood under the form of bread and wine. He made *The Twelve* priests of the New Testament, commanding them and their successors: "Do this for my Commemoration", as the Church has always understood and taught. And so, having celebrated with the Twelve at the Last Supper the memory of the first Passover from the slavery of Egypt to freedom, Christ established a new Passover: the Sacrifice of Himself, the true Lamb of God, to be sacramentally renewed by the Church through her priests in memory of His own passing over from this world to the Father, when He redeemed us by the shedding of His blood.

On the altar at every Mass, after the words of Consecration are uttered, lies the Body and Blood of Christ, still looking like bread and wine, but in outward appearance only. This mystery has been called transubstantiation. Christ becomes present on the altar as He now is in Heaven: not a dead body, but the glorious, risen Body; the True God and True Man, wholly and substantially present—Body, Blood, Soul and Divinity—under the veil of each species, in the smallest fragment and the tiniest drop.

The Mass is also the act of perfect worship offered to God: an offering of thanksgiving and praise. From Apostolic times the Mass came to be described as the *Eucharist*, derived from the Greek verb "to give thanks". When Christ died on the Cross, he offered the one and only sacrifice worthy of God, superseding the sacrificial offerings of animals. This sacrifice, offered by Christ alone, was perfect and no other could add to it, but it is Christ's wish that we who are members of his Mystical Body should be able to take part in this sacrifice and make our own offering of it to the Father. And so we join our self-offering to Christ's; this is what we do in the Mass. It is the sacrifice of the Church. It is also offered, as the Preface of each Mass reminds us, together with the Angels and Saints who stand in the presence of God. And finally, each Mass is the greatest prayer to be offered for the benefit of the living and the dead.

The Council of Trent (Session 22, Chapter V) reminds us that the Church, in accordance with apostolic discipline and tradition, has made use of ceremonies and instituted certain rites (such as mystical blessings, lights, incense, vestments, and many other things of this kind), so that the majesty of so great a sacrifice might be emphasised and the minds of the faithful excited by those visible signs of religion and piety to the contemplation of those most sublime things which are hidden in this sacrifice.

The sacredness of the altar

A full understanding of the nature of the Mass also involves an appreciation of the nature of the altar. "The altar of holy Church is Christ, as John testifies, when he says in his Apocalypse that he saw him as a golden altar standing before the throne. In him and through him the gifts of the faithful are offered to God the Father." This extract from the Roman Pontifical for the conferral of the office of subdeacon elucidates the Church's teaching that the altars of our churches signify Christ, although Christ himself is at the same time the priest who offers the Sacrifice, the sacrificial Victim and the Altar of Sacrifice. The altar, on which this great and mysterious Sacrifice is offered as the supreme act of the worship of God, demands respect.

The primacy of the altar in our devotion to the most holy Eucharist must never be forgotten, as the distinguished theologian and liturgist, Canon A. Croegart, emphasises: "Without the eucharistic sacrifice, there would be no communion; without communion, there would be no reserved sacrament, nor any of the other forms of devotion connected with the worship of the reserved sacrament. Everything depends upon the altar, yet this order of importance is all too frequently ignored." His conclusion is obvious, yet startling: "The altar is not an ornament of the church, but rather, the church is an architectural ornament housing and covering the altar. The jewel does not exist for the casket, but the casket is adapted to and serves the jewel." (August Croegaert, *The Mass*, vol. 1.) Consequently, our attitude to the altar should reflect a respect for its essential character and sacredness. The altar should not be touched and nothing should be placed upon it, save those things required for the celebration of Mass, and then only by the celebrant and his ministers.

The Structure of the Latin Mass

What is this Rite of Mass? This is the Mass which was normally celebrated throughout the Western Church up until 1970. It has been referred to in several different ways (e.g. "the Traditional Latin Mass", "the Old Mass", etc.), but is usually referred to as the Tridentine Mass, because the Roman Missal was first published by Pope Saint Pius V, at the specific request of the Fathers of the Council of Trent in the sixteenth century (the adjective *Tridentine* is derived from the name of the city of Trent). It is important to recall, however, that what Pius V published in 1570 was a Missal based upon the continuous liturgical practice of the Church since the time of Pope Saint Gregory the Great in the sixth century. Pope Benedict XVI in his motu proprio *Summorum Pontificum* has referred to this Mass as an *Extraordinary Form*, or *More Ancient Use* of the Roman Rite.

Over the course of the centuries, organically, since the time of the Apostles, various prayers and ceremonies were added to the Roman Rite of Mass.

Parts of it are very ancient: the Collects were composed before the fifth century and are believed to be the work of Popes Saint Damasus (366–84) and Leo the Great (440–461); the Canon of the Mass is believed to have been arranged, in part, by Saint Ambrose, bishop of Milan, in the fourth century, but the Preface and Sanctus and the Anamnesis are much older, whilst the formula of Consecration is (as one would expect) the oldest of all. The sequence of readings (which differs from the three cycles of the New Order of Mass) was set by the ninth century (but in the main by the sixth), although parts of it probably were arranged by Saint Jerome (d. 420). The Lord's Prayer and the Embolism which follows it, were set in place by Pope Saint Gregory the Great (590–604), although the use of the Lord's Prayer goes back, of course, to the earliest days of the Church. Other prayers were added somewhat later: the Prayers at the foot of the altar (between the eleventh and fourteenth centuries); the Offertory Prayers (fourteenth century); the Beginning of the Gospel of John at the conclusion of Mass (sixteenth century, although in some places it had been recited centuries before this). The ceremonies of this Rite—as distinct from the prayers—are recognisable from the sixth century.

Until 1965, the Mass had been entirely in Latin, but after the Second Vatican Council (and even before it in Germany and certain other countries), vernacular language (according to the spoken language of each nation) was introduced into the Mass in stages. Significant structural changes and the complete use of the vernacular were introduced in 1970 with the publication of the New Order of Mass by Pope Paul VI.

In 1984, and again in 1988, Pope John Paul II issued decrees which entitled bishops to authorise the celebration of this form of the Latin Mass again in their dioceses and he established the Ecclesia Dei Commission as a reference point for bishops, priests and the faithful in their "rightful aspiration" for this ancient liturgy. Pope Benedict XVI further clarified this by his motu proprio *Summorum Pontificum* of July 2007. These decrees require that the Roman Missal of 1962 (and associated liturgical books) be used for the celebration of such Masses. Certain changes to the rubrics (the regulations for the celebration of the Sacred Liturgy) of the Roman Missal were introduced in 1960, which are still binding upon the celebration of this Mass, whereas changes introduced into the Mass after 1964 are not binding. For the celebration of this Mass, *Summorum Pontificum* also granted permission for the Scripture to be read in the vernacular, for prefaces from the 1970 Missal to be used and for the Feasts of Saints canonized since 1962 to be commemorated. The Ecclesia Dei Commission also occasionally makes decisions touching on various aspects of the celebration of this liturgy. This Mass-book has been prepared in the light of all these permissions and requirements.

The rubrics of the 1962 Roman Missal refer to two kinds of Masses, Sung (or High Mass) and Low Mass. A Sung Mass is described as a Solemn Mass if the celebrant is assisted by a deacon and a subdeacon. "A Mass is High if the celebrating priest actually sings the parts prescribed by the rubrics to be sung by him; otherwise it is called Low Mass" (rubric no. 271). What needs to be emphasised immediately is that the **usual form of Mass** envisaged for the 1962 Missal is the **Sung Mass**. The ancient traditions of the Church have always assumed that Mass is to be sung. It should be added that the rules for Low Mass are derived from the rules for High Mass. In the restoration of the More Ancient Use of the Roman Rite, it is important that the Church's expectation of the liturgy being sung whenever possible, be respected, whatever the experience of the past might have been.

The **Low** Mass had its origins as a private Mass, celebrated by a priest, assisted by one minister: no congregation was present. Furthermore, from the earliest days of the Church, the Funeral liturgy was often celebrated without singing at the place of entombment. As the liturgy of the Church changed at the beginning of the Middle Ages and as the number of priests in any one diocese increased, churches began to have several altars for the celebration of Mass. This was more especially so in Monastic communities. Whereas at this time, the principal Mass of the Parish was sung solemnly with the ancient chants of the Church, priests would celebrate other Masses privately, saying rather than singing them. After the time of the "Reformation" in the sixteenth century, the practice of the Catholic Faith became a criminal offence in England and Ireland: Masses had to be celebrated secretly and silently. Where the Faith was brought to the New World by English and Irish Catholics, the long-lasting effects of the persecution was reflected in the celebration of Mass. Missionary conditions, moreover, often prevented more solemn celebrations of the Liturgy. This extremely simplified history accounts for why so few parishes before the Second Vatican Council knew the Sung Mass.

Whether in sung or said form, the More Ancient Use of the Roman Rite is divided into two parts, the **Mass of the Catechumens** and the **Mass of the Faithful**. These two names reflect the practice of the early Church whereby those preparing for baptism were permitted to attend the first part of the Mass, but were excluded from the principal part of the Mass. Consequently the **Mass of the Catechumens** may be considered a preparation. Its equivalent in the 1970 Missal is the Liturgy of the Word. It consists of the celebrant's private prayers and confession at the foot of the altar, the Introit, Kyrie eleison, the Gloria, the Collect, the Epistle, Gospel and Creed (on Sundays and greater Feasts).

The principal part of the Mass, known as the **Mass of the Faithful**, commences with the celebrant's offering of bread and wine and the Secret Prayer; the Preface follows, leading to the Canon of the Mass in which bread and wine are transubstantiated into the Body and Blood of Christ. Holy Communion is preceded by the Lord's Prayer. The Mass concludes with the Postcommunion prayer, the celebrant's blessing and the beginning of the Gospel of John.

The ethos of the Latin Mass

In 1970, when the New Order of Mass was introduced, much was changed pertaining to the celebration of Mass and everything associated with it. The nature of the Mass, of course, did not change, but how it was presented changed very markedly. It was far more than a change from Latin to English: it involved a change in emphasis. In trying to simplify the Sacred Liturgy and make it more readily comprehensible, the architects of the New Order of Mass have emphasised the communal aspect of the Mass. Typically, the celebrant stands on one side of the altar, facing the congregation, and all are gathered around the table of the Lord, to partake of the Sacred Banquet. Very often there is a strong emphasis on active external participation.

When the celebrant is not facing the congregation, however, the entire atmosphere of the Mass is changed: both priest and people are facing the same direction to pray. Many have forgotten that from earliest Christian times, Mass was celebrated looking towards the rising sun (a great symbol of the Resurrection, and of Christ's Second Coming in Glory): everyone faced this direction. Furthermore, the Mass is not limited to the confines of the building in which it is being celebrated, but is a cosmic event, involving the angels and saints and the souls of the faithful departed who are yet to receive their eternal reward. Simply by changing the position of the celebrant, a different sense of the Mass as a sacred event is conveyed to all present. The great silences, the solemn ritual actions of the celebrant and the beauty of the ancient Latin prayers, all reinforce the mysterious and sacred atmosphere of this More Ancient Use of the Roman Mass.

The sense of the sacred is not only manifest in the celebration of the Liturgy itself, but in all the things that surround it: the way the celebrant is vested, the manner in which the altar is decorated, the manner in which the celebrant and his ministers conduct themselves in the sanctuary—all of these things are governed by rules which the Church in her wisdom adopted over the course of centuries.

The celebrant vests in an **amice**, which covers his shoulders and neck, a long white robe called an **alb**, which he ties with a cord called a **cincture**. He places a small vestment over his left arm called a **maniple** (originally a cloth used to wipe his mouth and brow) and around his neck the symbol of his priestly authority, the **stole**. Over all these, he vests in the **chasuble**. The vestments, designed for use in the Sacred Liturgy, are required to be blessed. The colour of these vestments varies according to the liturgical season or feast: violet and purple for Advent and Lent; white for Christmas, Easter and Saints' days; red for Pentecost and for the Apostles and Martyrs; green for the time before Lent and after Pentecost; rose for the mid-point Sundays of Advent and Lent and black for Masses of the dead.

Just as the celebrant puts on vestments for the Sacred Liturgy, so, too, the chalice and the altar are vested. The altar, which signifies Christ himself and upon which the Sacrifice of the Mass is offered, is vested in a frontal which matches the colour of the celebrant's vestments. Upon the altar, three cloths made of linen rest. In the middle of the altar a large Cross is placed between the candlesticks. The number of candles is graded according to the solemnity of the occasion, two, four or six.

The Church has regulated all these things, in order to create a certain image around and to preserve a certain attitude to the Mass. There are other things concerning the More Ancient Use of the Roman Rite about which the Church has made certain regulations; such things are also designed to preserve the sacredness of the Mass and the sanctuary where it is celebrated. At this form of Mass, those receiving Holy Communion must do so on the tongue, **not in the hand**. Unless there is some disability, those receiving Holy Communion should kneel before the altar at the Communion rail. The same laws of fasting which govern the New Order of Mass also govern the More Ancient Use of the Roman Mass.

Participation in the Latin Mass

One of the major differences between the New Order of Mass and the More Ancient Use concerns the active participation of those in attendance. Concerning participation, the rubrics of the 1962 Roman Missal say: "The Mass of its nature demands that all present at it should share in it in the way proper to each one. The various ways in which the faithful may actually share in the Mass should be so ordered that the danger of any abuse should be removed, and the chief purpose of such participation should be attained, i.e., the fuller worship of God and the edification of the faithful." Some have the impression that participation means doing or saying something, but, of course, it is possible to make all the responses at Mass without any form of attentiveness to what is taking place. One of the last decrees issued by Pope Pius XII in 1958 makes the important point that "participation should above all be interior—consisting in devout attention of mind and the affections of the heart. The faithful thereby enter into closest union with their High Priest ... and together with him and through him offer the Sacrifice, surrendering themselves in union with him" (*Instruction of the Congregation of Sacred Rites on Sacred Music and the Sacred Liturgy,* 3rd September, 1958). This document goes on to speak of the secondary form of participation at Mass: "The participation of those present becomes more complete, however, when in addition to this interior attention there is an outward participation, manifesting itself in outward acts. These include bodily posture (kneeling, standing, sitting), ceremonial gestures and especially responses, prayers and singing."

One of the greater strengths of the More Ancient Use of the Roman Rite is its balance. For those who feel able to pray best in the silence of their hearts, there is room; for those who desire to respond to the liturgical greetings of the celebrant, there is room; there is a balance between standing, kneeling and sitting as is appropriate for each part of the Mass and in accord with ancient practices. This booklet is devised with all these things in mind. The rules regarding sitting, standing and kneeling were revised in the 1962 Roman Missal to make for a greater similarity between the rules for Low Mass (particularly for the dialogue Mass in its various degrees) and the rules for the Sung Mass. Previously, the congregation was required to kneel throughout Low Mass, except to stand for the Gospel. This arrangement, which only appeared around the time of the "Reformation" and which was derived from the actions of the server (who in Masses without congregations knelt throughout), took little account of the more solemn and less solemn parts of the Mass, nor of the ancient practices of standing for the singing of the Collect, the Preface and the Lord's Prayer. This book makes explicit when the congregation should stand, kneel or sit, based upon the rubrical revision of 1962; the directions apply equally to Low Mass (particularly a parish or community Mass) and to the Sung Mass.

There is also provision now for the congregation to respond to the greetings of the celebrant, and to pray with the celebrant (where it is customary) the Lord's Prayer (in Latin) in accordance with regulations issued by Pope Pius XII in 1958. At a Sung Mass and where it is customary, the Lord's Prayer may be chanted by the celebrant and the congregation all together, in accordance with previous permissions of the Congregation of Sacred Rites and confirmed by a decision of the Ecclesia Dei Commission. The occasions for the congregation to respond to the celebrant are **few** and not difficult; furthermore, the minister makes some of the responses alone. No one is required to respond, but when the celebrant greets the congregation with the words "Dominus vobiscum", it is appropriate that all respond to him, just as all respond in the Prayers after Low Mass. The responses which the congregation may make are clearly marked in this book.

DEVOTIONAL PRAYERS BEFORE MASS

A Prayer before Mass

Eternal Father, I offer you the Sacrifice wherein your dear Son, Jesus, offered himself upon the Cross and which he now renews upon this altar:

To adore you and to render to you that honour which is your due, acknowledging your supreme dominion over all things and their absolute dependence upon you, for you are our first beginning and our last end;

To give you thanks for countless benefits received;

To appease your justice, provoked to anger by so many sins and to offer you worthy satisfaction for them;

And finally to implore your grace and mercy for myself, for all those who are in tribulation and distress, for all poor sinners, for the whole world and for the blessed souls in purgatory. Amen.

For sinners
(Rite of Evesham, 13th century)

O God, in whose sight every soul may well fear and every conscience tremble, be gracious to every cry of sorrow and heal the wounds of sins in all. Even as none of us is free from fault, so may none be stranger to your mercy. Amen.

For the Church
(Missal of Robert of Jumieges, 11th century)

Almighty, Eternal God, by ever giving strength to our weakness, you enable the Church to flourish even amidst its trials, so that when it appears to men to be utterly cast down, then rather does it gloriously prevail. Whilst, then, it accepts affliction as a proving of its faith, let it persevere, by your grace, in triumphant loyalty. Amen.

For the faithful
(Anselm of Bury Saint Edmund's, 12th century)

To all who live by the truths of the faith give grace, most tender Father, that they may lead upright and holy lives, never departing from your teaching. To those who as yet have not found faith in you, grant that before they quit this life they may believe and know the love of your holy name. Then, having known it, may they keep it firm and inviolate. Let the Sacrifice of your Body and Blood win pardon of sins for the living and the dead. Amen.

Prayers in Preparation for Holy Communion

(Saint Anselm, 12th century)

O Lord Jesus Christ, by the desire of the Father and the co-operating of the Holy Spirit, you willingly and mercifully redeemed the world from sin and from eternal death. Though it be with lowly devotion, and all too little love, yet it is with thankfulness for so great a grace and to the best of my power that I desire to receive, to the cleansing of my soul and as a defence against sin, your sacred Body and Blood. But my confidence is all in that loving-kindness by which, that sinners might find grace, you offered and laid down your life as a sacrifice to the Father. Therefore do I dare, sinner though I be, to receive these holy gifts that through them I may find holiness. . . . Make me, O Lord, so to receive your gifts on my lips and into my heart with such feelings of faith and love that, by their power and my own repentance and renewed goodness of life, I may have some likeness to your death and resurrection. So may I be a worthy member of your body which is the Church, that I may also be a member of you, that you may live in me and I in you. Amen.

(Jeremy Taylor, 17th century)

Lord, you have prepared a banquet for me against those who trouble me: let that holy sacrament of the Eucharist be to me a defence and shield, a nourishment and medicine, life and health, a means of sanctification and spiritual growth; that I, receiving the body of my dearest Lord, may be one with his mystical body and of the same spirit, united with indissoluble bonds of a strong faith and a holy hope and a never-failing charity, that from beneath this veil I may pass into the visions of eternal clarity, from eating your body to beholding your face in the glories of your everlasting kingdom, O blessed and eternal Jesus. Amen.

A Prayer to the Blessed Virgin Mary

O Mother of Mercy, most Blessed Virgin Mary, I, all unworthy, have recourse to you with heartfelt love and confidence. As you stood by your Son while he was offering himself on the Cross, be pleased to stand by me and by all who are offering Mass this day. May we, by your gracious help, offer a worthy and acceptable sacrifice in the sight of God. Amen.

THE MASS OF THE CATECHUMENS

The Mass of the Catechumens is so called because, in the early Church, those preparing for Baptism (designated catechumens), were permitted to attend this part of the Mass. The Bidding Prayers or Prayers of the Faithful, denoted that point at which the catechumens were dismissed with the words *Ite missa est* (Go, it is the dismissal). It is from this phrase that our word Mass is derived. Although the Mass of the Catechumens was always penitential in character, the later addition of the psalm with its antiphon Introibo ad altare Dei, the Confiteor and the Kyrie emphasise the need to approach the altar in a spirit of recollection, cleansing our hearts before offering worship to God.

The Asperges

The *Asperges* began as an early monastic practice, when the church, the monastery and all those gathered for the Sunday Mass would be sprinkled with holy water. Essentially, the use of holy water reflects the concern of the Church for the purification of the soul before the celebration of the Mass. As such, it is a suitable complement to the penitential character of the Preparatory prayers. The sprinkling with holy water reminds us of our Baptism, by means of which we were freed from original sin, and any actual sin, and adopted as children of God. Having intoned the penitential psalm *Miserere*, the celebrant sprinkles the altar with holy water, then himself and the ministers. He moves through the church sprinkling the congregation. The sign of the Cross is made whilst being sprinkled with holy water. In Paschaltide, the sprinkling of Holy Water is accompanied by the chant *Vidi aquam*. As the ceremony occurs only at the principal Mass on Sunday, on other occasions when we enter the church, it is customary to take Holy Water from the stoup ordinarily provided at the entrance.

The Prayers at the foot of the altar

The celebrant prepares for Mass with a series of psalms and prayers, the last of which he recites after processing to the altar, but before going up to it. Consequently, these final prayers are referred to as the Prayers at the foot of the altar. Of a somewhat later origin, initially they were recited by the celebrant on his way from the sacristy to the altar. Accordingly, they are most properly regarded as the private prayers of the celebrant and the ministers. At a Sung Mass, the choir sings the *Introit* as the celebrant and ministers process to the altar: this chanting continues until the celebrant and ministers have concluded the Prayers at the foot of the altar. The excerpt from Psalm 42 is not recited in Masses for the Dead, nor during Passiontide, which reflects its relatively late addition to the Mass.

The Confiteor

Although we are accustomed to regard the forgiveness of our sins as a matter between ourselves and God, the Church teaches that sin effects the entire Body of Christ. And so the *Confiteor* is not only an admission of our guilt to God, but also a mutual confession of our sinfulness. Furthermore, it shows the involvement of the Saints in the work of our forgiveness, for we also confess our guilt to them who then intercede for us with the eternal Judge to obtain pardon for our sins. Consequently, the Confiteor is an important and practical reminder to us of the doctrine of the Communion of Saints. Public confession is also a sacramental, which enables us to obtain from God the remission of our venial sins, through the merits of our Lord Jesus Christ.

The kissing of the altar

The prayer *Oramus te, Domine* makes evident that the kissing of the altar is primarily an act of veneration of the relics of the saints contained there in the altar stone. For the More Ancient Use, the Church prescribes that every altar shall contain relics of the martyrs. In pagan antiquity it was customary to kiss thresholds of temples, symbols of gods and altars, but the Church took over this custom at an early date and greeted their own Christian altars in the same way. This prayer also relates to the Roman practice of offering Mass at the tombs of the martyrs, in the catacombs.

The *Introit* is an entrance-chant to inspire appropriate thoughts and sentiments with which to begin the Mass of the Day. The antiphon gives the main thought; the significance of the middle verse must be looked for in the psalm from which it is extracted.

The Introit

Pope Gelasius I (died 496) took the litany (a form of intercession used in the Eastern Liturgy) with its oft-repeated response *Kyrie eleison*, and placed it at the beginning of the ancient Roman liturgy, before the readings from the scripture. The litany was considerably shortened by Pope Gregory the Great, reducing it merely to the response Kyrie eleison, to which was added *Christe, eleison*, musically elaborated by the choir. This short prayer to Christ (the only remnant of those earliest days when the liturgy was celebrated in Greek rather than Latin) by its brevity and repetitions evokes an urgency and reminds us yet again that in entering upon the Sacrifice of the Mass we must be mindful of our unworthiness and raise our hearts to God.

The Kyrie

This sublime chant is at the same time both simple in its language and profound in its doctrine and feeling. Once referred to as not so much a hymn as a series of inspired acclamations addressed to Christ, the *Gloria* was used as a prayer in Greek and in Latin as early as the fourth century, but by the fifth century it made its appearance in the Roman liturgy, and then only in the Papal Dawn Mass of Christmas. The introduction is the song of the angels, heralding to the shepherds the birth of Christ, as recorded in Saint Luke's Gospel. The first verses are an acclamation of praise and thanksgiving to God the Father, whilst that which follows them, addressed to God the Son, is both a prayer of praise and intercession. Lastly, mention is made of the Holy Spirit, who, somewhat briefly, is praised together with the Father and the Son.

The Gloria

The celebrant venerates the altar (the symbol of Christ, from whom comes every saving grace) with a kiss and by that kiss he receives from Christ the strength of grace. Then he turns to the people with his hands outstretched and says *Dominus vobiscum,* and by so doing, imparts to those assembled the grace which he himself has received from his veneration of the altar. This ancient and frequently-used greeting originated in the traditional forms of greeting found in the Old Testament. By it, the celebrant (or deacon) solemnly greets the people of God, who, in responding, acknowledge the power of holy

The Greeting

orders which he possesses. Only a bishop. possessed of the fulness of Christ's priesthood, may address the people with the evangelical greeting of Christ himself: *Pax vobis.*

The *Collect* is a community prayer, the celebrant recites it for the people and in their name, collecting together and concluding the petitions of all. It brings to a conclusion all that precedes it, whilst providing an introduction to the readings from scripture which follow. The prayer is always introduced with the word *Oremus.* The Collect is answered with the word *Amen*: it is our declaration of approval and unity with the words of the celebrant. This word is from the Hebrew and means "so be it" and it may be found in all ancient Jewish and early Christian liturgies. The *Dominus vobiscum*, the *Oremus* and the *Amen* unite the celebrant and people together and make of the Collect a prayer which is in very truth the prayer of the people. The Collects are amongst the very oldest prayers of the Mass and are renowned for their beautiful and restrained style. They are mostly addressed to the Father and are based upon the mediation of the Son. The conclusion of the prayer "in the unity of the Holy Spirit" perfects its Trinitarian character. The words of the Collect bear much consideration and are very suitable for our daily prayer.

The reading of the Scripture at Mass is a practice which goes back to the beginnings of Christianity, having its origins in Jewish Synagogue worship (refer Luke 4:16–20 and Acts 13:15). But the arrangement of readings in the 1962 Missal does not reflect the primitive sequence, but rather the result of many alterations, additions and other unusual factors over several centuries. Originally, the Roman Rite had three readings (certain ferial and penitential days still have three or more readings). The *Gradual* chant followed the Old Testament reading and the Alleluia the epistles, but then these chants came to follow one after the other. As with the *Introit*, *Offertorium* and *Communio* the selection of psalms for the Gradual was determined by the scripture it accompanies. The ancient practice was to sing the lessons from a raised reading desk called an Ambo. In a sung Mass, where it is customary, this ancient practice for the singing of the Scripture may still be observed.

The Gospel is not merely an instruction, nor yet merely the climax of the instructive part of the Mass of the Catechumens: it is much more. The liturgy is not so much concerned with giving instruction in the Gospel narratives, as with drawing a mystical parallel between Christ's chronicled works and deeds and how Christ works in the Eucharist. The special function of the Gospel is frequently to serve as a bridge, which leads us directly to the Holy Sacrifice. The liturgy also sees in the Gospel the presence of Christ himself, and its proclamation is an act of homage paid to Christ. Furthermore, the ceremonies surrounding that proclamation mark it as the most solemn part of the Mass of the Catechumens. This is evident at a sung Mass, when candles and incense are used. At the Solemn Mass, however, when the deacon and subdeacon assist, the Liturgy's emphasis on the proclamation of the Gospel is made most clear. During the chanting of the Gradual, the deacon places upon the altar the Book of the Gospels and then kneels to receive the blessing of the celebrant. The deacon, with the Book of Gospels and accompanied by the subdeacon and preceded by ministers bearing incense and candles, goes to the northern side of the sanctuary or to the Ambo. There, whilst the subdeacon holds the Book of Gospels, he sings the Gospel, flanked by the candle-bearers. All stand and turn to face the Book of the Gospels. After the Eastward orientation of prayer at the altar, this is the most important bodily orientation at Mass. By it, we recognise Christ speaking to us in the Gospel and we undertake to turn our whole lives to him. Afterwards, the subdeacon takes the Book of Gospels to the celebrant at the altar, who kisses it. This elaborate and beautiful ceremonial surrounds the mystery that it is Christ who speaks in the Gospel and it is Christ who is honoured by it. Until the middle ages, the ceremonial surrounding the proclamation of the Gospel was even more elaborate and afterward all present kissed the Book of Gospels (although only the clergy kissed its opened pages, saying "By the words of the gospel may our sins be wiped away"). These ceremonies are very ancient. The procession with the Book, candles and incense is known to have existed by the seventh century, but the customs of standing for the Gospel, placing the Book of Gospels on the altar and kissing the Book go back even further and have always been regarded as signs of respect and worship. The three small signs of the Cross made as the Gospel is announced signify that the Gospel must be grasped by our minds, proclaimed by our lips and treasured in our hearts.

This is the Creed of the First Council of Nicea (A.D. 325) enlarged by the Council of Constantinople (A.D. 381). It was drawn up to refute the heretical teachings of a priest of Alexandria, Arius, concerning the divinity of Christ. It stresses in every way the divine nature of Christ, his universal sovereignty, his one-ness of substance with the Father. All of the clauses of the Creed were formulated so as to make it perfectly explicit what the Church believed concerning God, Father, Son and Holy Spirit. These words were forged in an age of terrible divisions within the Church: many thousands of bishops, priests and people came to be misled by the false teachings of Arius during and after his lifetime. When professing our faith with these words, we should reflect upon the meaning of each and every phrase.

The Creed

The Asperges

You will sprinkle me, O Lord, with hyssop, and I shall be cleansed; you will wash me and I shall become whiter than snow. Have mercy on me, O God, according to your great mercy.

Glory be to the Father, and to the Son, and to the Holy Spirit. As it was in the beginning, is now and ever shall be, throughout all ages. Amen.

Antiphon: Asperges me, Domine, hyssopo, et mundabor: lavabis me, et super nivem dealbabor.
Miserere mei, Deus, secundum magnam misericordiam tuam.
Gloria Patri, et Filio, et Spiritui Sancto.
Sicut erat in principio, et nunc, et semper, et in saecula saeculorum. Amen.

But during the Season of Easter:

I saw water flowing from the right side of the temple, alleluia; and all to whom that water came were saved and sang: alleluia, alleluia.

Praise the Lord, for he is good: for his mercy endures for ever.

Glory be to the Father, and to the Son, and to the Holy Spirit. As it was in the beginning, is now and ever shall be, throughout all ages. Amen.

Antiphon: Vidi aquam egredientem de templo, a latere dextro, alleluia: et omnes ad quos pervenit aqua ista salvi facti sunt, et dicent: alleluia, alleluia.
Confitemini Domino, quoniam bonus: quoniam in saeculum misericordia ejus.
Gloria Patri, et Filio, et Spiritui Sancto. Sicut erat in principio, et nunc, et semper, et in saecula saeculorum. Amen.

Celebrant: Ostende nobis, Domine, misericordiam tuam.

ALL RESPOND: **Et salutare tuum da nobis.**

C. Domine, exaudi orationem meam.

ALL RESPOND: **Et clamor meus ad te veniat.**

C. Dominus vobiscum.

ALL RESPOND: **Et cum spiritu tuo.**

C. Oremus.

The celebrant sings the Oration:

Exaudi nos, Domine sancte, Pater omnipotens, aeterne Deus, et mittere digneris sanctum Angelum tuum de caelis, qui custodiat, foveat, protegat, visitet, atque defendat omnes habitantes in hoc habitaculo. Per Christum Dominum nostrum.

Hear us, O holy Lord, almighty Father, eternal God, and be pleased to send your holy Angel from heaven to guard, assist, protect, defend and extend your favour toward all who are assembled in this place. Through Christ our Lord.

ALL RESPOND: **Amen.**

At the Foot of the Altar

PRAYERS AT THE FOOT OF THE ALTAR

As the procession moves towards the altar, all stand. The celebrant and his ministers quietly recite the Prayers at the foot of the altar, beginning with the Sign of the Cross. During a Sung Mass, the choir continues with the singing of the Introit.

KNEEL

In nomine ✠ Patris, et Filii, et Spiritus Sancti. Amen.

Introibo ad altare Dei.

Minister: Ad Deum qui laetificat juventutem meam.

C. Judica me, Deus, et discerne causam meam de gente non sancta: ab homine iniquo et doloso erue me.

M. Quia tu es, Deus, fortitudo mea: quare me repulisti, et quare tristis incedo, dum affligit me inimicus?

C. Emitte lucem tuam, et veritatem tuam: ipsa me deduxerunt, et adduxerunt in montem sanctum tuum, et in tabernacula tua.

M. Et introibo ad altare Dei: ad Deum qui laetificat juventutem meam.

C. Confitebor tibi in cithara Deus, Deus meus: quare tristis es, anima mea, et quare conturbas me?

M. Spera in Deo, quoniam adhuc confitebor illi: salutare vultus mei, et Deus meus.

C. Gloria Patri, et Filio, et Spiritui Sancto.

M. Sicut erat in principio et nunc, et semper, et in saecula saeculorum. Amen.

C. Introibo ad altare Dei.

M. Ad Deum qui laetificat juventutem meam.

C. ✠ Adjutorium nostrum in nomine Domini.

M. Qui fecit caelum et terram.

C. In the name of the Father, and of the Son and of the Holy Spirit. Amen.

I will go up to God's altar.

M. To God, who gives me joy as in the days of my youth.

C. Vindicate me, O God, and defend my cause against an ungodly people; from the unjust and deceitful deliver me.

M. For you, O God, are my stronghold: why do you cast me away? Why should I go away in sadness oppressed by the enemy?

C. Send forth your light and your truth to lead me and bring me to your holy mountain, to the place where you dwell.

M. And I will go up to God's altar, to God who gives me joy as in the days of my youth.

C. I shall sing thanks to you upon the harp, O God, my God. But why are you downcast, my soul, why are you stirred up within me?

M. Hope in God! I shall continue to praise him: my Saviour, and my God.

C. Glory be to the Father, and to the Son, and to the Holy Spirit.

M. As it was in the beginning, is now, and ever shall be, throughout all ages. Amen.

C. I will go up to God's altar.

M. To God, who gives me joy as in the days of my youth.

C. Our help is in the name of the Lord.

M. Who made heaven and earth.

Bowing low, the celebrant makes his Confession, after which the minister responds:

C. I confess to almighty God...

M. May almighty God have mercy on you, forgive you your sins, and bring you to life everlasting.

C. Amen.

M. Misereatur tui omnipotens Deus, et, dimissis peccatis tuis, perducat te ad vitam aeternam.

C. Amen.

Then the minister makes the Confession to the celebrant:

I confess to almighty God, to blessed Mary ever Virgin, to blessed Michael the Archangel, to blessed John the Baptist, to the holy Apostles Peter and Paul, to all the Saints, and to you, Father, that I have sinned exceedingly, in thought, word and deed, through my fault, through my fault, through my most grievous fault. Therefore, I beseech blessed Mary ever Virgin, blessed Michael the Archangel, blessed John the Baptist, the holy Apostles Peter and Paul, all the Saints, and you, Father, to pray to the Lord our God for me.

Confiteor Deo omnipotenti, beatae Mariae semper Virgini, beato Michaeli Archangelo, beato Joanni Baptistae, sanctis Apostolis Petro et Paulo, omnibus Sanctis, et tibi, Pater: quia peccavi nimis cogitatione, verbo et opere (*he strikes his breast three times*) mea culpa, mea culpa, mea maxima culpa. Ideo precor beatam Mariam semper Virginem, beatum Michaelem Archangelum, beatum Joannem Baptistam, sanctos Apostolos Petrum et Paulum, omnes Sanctos, et te, Pater, orare pro me ad Dominum Deum nostrum.

C. May almighty God have mercy upon you, forgive you your sins, and bring you to life everlasting.

M. Amen.

C. Misereatur vestri omnipotens Deus, et dimissis peccatis vestris, perducat vos ad vitam aeternam.

M. Amen.

C. May the almighty and merciful Lord grant us pardon, absolution, and remission of our sins.

M. Amen.

C. Turn to us, O God, and give us life,

M. And your people will rejoice in you.

C. Show us, Lord, your mercy.

M. And grant us your salvation.

C. Lord, hear my prayer.

M. And let my cry come to you.

C. The Lord be with you.

M. And with your spirit.

C. ✠ Indulgentiam, absolutionem, et remissionem peccatorum nostrorum tribuat nobis omnipotens et misericors Dominus.

M. Amen.

C. Deus, tu conversus vivificabis nos.

M. Et plebs tua laetabitur in te.

C. Ostende nobis, Domine, misericordiam tuam.

M. Et salutare tuum da nobis.

C. Domine, exaudi orationem meam.

M. Et clamor meus ad te veniat.

C. Dominus vobiscum.

to which the minister alone responds:

Et cum spiritu tuo.

Oremus.   C. Let us pray.

The celebrant goes up to the altar; at a Sung Mass, he incenses the altar.   **STAND**

Aufer a nobis, quaesumus, Domine, iniquitates nostras: ut ad Sancta sanctorum puris mereamur mentibus introire. Per Christum Dominum nostrum. Amen.

Oramus te, Domine, per merita Sanctorum tuorum, quorum reliquiae hic sunt, et omnium Sanctorum: ut indulgere digneris omnia peccata mea. Amen.

Take away our sins from us, we beseech you, O Lord; that we may be worthy to enter the holy of holies with pure hearts. Through Christ our Lord. Amen.

We beseech you, O Lord, through the merits of your Saints, whose relics rest here, and of all the Saints, that you may be pleased to pardon all my sins. Amen.

THE INTROIT AND KYRIE

At a Sung Mass, the choir chants the Introit. All join in singing the Kyrie and Gloria.

(THE PROPER OF THE MASS FOR THE DAY)

Celebrant: Kyrie, eleison

ALL RESPOND: **Kyrie, eleison**

Celebrant: Kyrie, eleison

ALL RESPOND: **Christe, eleison**

Celebrant: Christe, eleison

ALL RESPOND: **Christe, eleison**

Celebrant: Kyrie, eleison

ALL RESPOND: **Kyrie, eleison**

Celebrant: Kyrie, eleison.

THE GLORIA AND COLLECT

Gloria in excelsis Deo,
et in terra pax hominibus bonae voluntatis.
Laudamus te.
Benedicimus te.
Adoramus te.
Glorificamus te.
Gratias agimus tibi
propter magnam gloriam tuam:
Domine Deus, Rex caelestis,
Deus Pater omnipotens.
Domine Fili unigenite, Jesu Christe;
Domine Deus, Agnus Dei, Filius Patris:
Qui tollis peccata mundi, miserere nobis;
Qui tollis peccata mundi,
suscipe deprecationem nostram;
Qui sedes ad dexteram Patris,
miserere nobis.
Quoniam tu solus Sanctus.
Tu solus Dominus.
Tu solus Altissimus, Jesu Christe.
✠ Cum Sancto Spiritu,
in gloria Dei Patris. Amen.

Glory be to God on high, and on earth peace to men of goodwill. We praise you, we bless you, we adore you, we glorify you, we give thanks to you for your great glory, Lord God, heavenly King, God the Father Almighty. Lord Jesus Christ, only-begotten Son, Lord God, Lamb of God, Son of the Father; you who take away the sins of the world, have mercy on us; you who take away the sins of the world, receive our prayer; you who sit at the right hand of the Father, have mercy on us. For you alone are holy; you alone are Lord; you alone, Jesus Christ, are the Most High, with the Holy Spirit, in the glory of God the Father. Amen.

Celebrant: Dominus vobiscum.

At a pontifical Mass, the bishop always greets the Faithful with the words: Pax vobis.

ALL RESPOND: **Et cum spiritu tuo.**

Celebrant: Oremus.

(THE PROPER OF THE MASS FOR THE DAY)

The Celebrant sings or says the Collect, which concludes with the words:

Celebrant: per omnia saecula saeculorum.

ALL RESPOND: **Amen.**

At the Gloria

THE SCRIPTURE

The Epistle, Gradual and Alleluia chants, the Gospel

(On penitential days, the Tract replaces the Alleluia chant.)

(THE PROPER OF THE MASS FOR THE DAY)

The celebrant (or at a Solemn Mass, the deacon) prepares for the Gospel:

Cleanse my heart and my lips, almighty God, who cleansed the lips of the Prophet Isaiah with a glowing coal: in your gracious mercy be pleased so to cleanse me, that I may worthily proclaim your holy Gospel.   Through Christ our Lord. Amen.

Munda cor meum ac labia mea, omnipotens Deus, qui labia Isaiae Prophetae calculo mundasti ignito: ita me tua grata miseratione dignare mundare, ut sanctum Evangelium tuum digne valeam nuntiare. Per Christum Dominum nostrum. Amen.

Lord (Sir), give the blessing.

May the Lord be in my (your) heart and on my (your) lips that I (you) may worthily and fittingly proclaim his Gospel. Amen.

Jube, Domine (Domne), benedicere.
Dominus sit in corde meo (tuo), et in labiis meis (tuis): ut digne et competenter annuntiem (annunties) Evangelium suum. Amen.

STAND

Celebrant or deacon: Dominus vobiscum.

ALL RESPOND: **Et cum spiritu tuo.**

Celebrant or deacon: Sequentia Sancti Evangelii secundum *[Joannem]*.

ALL RESPOND: **Gloria tibi Domine.**

(THE PROPER OF THE MASS FOR THE DAY)

The Gospel is read or sung.

A homily may be given after the Gospel. Please sit during the homily.

At the Creed

THE CREED

On Sundays and greater Feasts,
the celebrant recites the Creed; it is chanted by all at a Sung Mass.

Credo in unum Deum,
Patrem omnipotentem,
factorem caeli et terrae,
visibilium omnium et invisibilium.
Et in unum Dominum Jesum Christum,
Filium Dei unigenitum.
Et ex Patre natum ante omnia saecula.
Deum de Deo, lumen de lumine,
Deum verum de Deo vero.
Genitum, non factum,
consubstantialem Patri:
per quem omnia facta sunt.
Qui propter nos homines et propter nostram
salutem descendit de caelis.

All genuflect during the following words:

**Et incarnatus est de Spiritu Sancto
ex Maria Virgine et homo factus est.**

Crucifixus etiam pro nobis
sub Pontio Pilato passus et sepultus est.
Et resurrexit tertia die,
secundum Scripturas.
Et ascendit in caelum:
sedet ad dexteram Patris.
Et iterum venturus est cum gloria
judicare vivos, et mortuos:
cujus regni non erit finis.
Et in Spiritum Sanctum,
Dominum et vivificantem:
qui ex Patre, Filioque procedit.
Qui cum Patre, et Filio simul adoratur,
et conglorificatur
qui locutus est per Prophetas.
Et unam, sanctam, catholicam
et apostolicam Ecclesiam.
Confiteor unum baptisma
in remissionem peccatorum.
Et expecto resurrectionem mortuorum.
✠ Et vitam venturi saeculi. Amen.

I believe in one God, the Father almighty, the maker of heaven and earth, and of all things visible and invisible. I believe in one Lord, Jesus Christ, only-begotten Son of God, born of the Father before all ages. God from God, light from light, true God from true God. Begotten, not made, one in substance with the Father: through him all things were made. For us men and for our salvation, he came down from heaven;

By the Holy Spirit, he became incarnate of the Virgin Mary, and was made man.

He was crucified for us, suffered under Pontius Pilate, and was buried. On the third day, he rose again, according to the Scriptures. He ascended into heaven, and sits at the right hand of the Father. He will come again with glory to judge the living and the dead, and of his reign there will be no end. I believe in the Holy Spirit, the Lord and giver of life, who proceeds from the Father and the Son; who together with the Father and the Son, is adored and glorified; who spoke through the Prophets. And I believe in one, holy, catholic and apostolic Church. I acknowledge one baptism for the remission of sins. I await the resurrection of the dead, and the life of the world to come. Amen.

The Mass of the Faithful

The Mass of the Faithful (so called because in the early Church only those who were baptised were permitted to remain) can be divided into three distinct parts. Firstly, the Offertory, or preparation of the Sacrifice: the bread and wine are brought to the altar and offered to God with ceremonies and prayers, ending with the Secret prayer. Secondly, the Consecration, the moment of Sacrifice, introduced by the Preface and the Sanctus. The gifts of bread and wine become the Body and Blood of Christ. Finally, in the Communion, we receive back these gifts, now transubstantiated, and with them divine life. In preparation for Holy Communion, we say the Lord's Prayer; the Postcommunio and Blessing follow as a thanksgiving.

The *Offertorium* is a verse, generally taken from the Psalms or from some other book of the Scriptures. It is not concerned with the offering of bread and wine, but rather, gives expression to the dominant thought of the Mass of the Day; in short it has the same significance and purpose as the *Introit*, *Gradual* and *Communio*. In common with these three chants, the *Offertorium* was intended to be a musical accompaniment to a procession. From earliest times until the tenth or eleventh century, the faithful brought their gifts of bread and wine processionally to the altar, where they were received ceremonially by the celebrant and his ministers. The ministers poured the wine into the chalice and carried the bread to the altar upon a cloth. Although the procession fell into desuetude, a vestige of it can be seen in Solemn Mass when the subdeacon takes the chalice to the altar wrapped in a humeral veil.

The gifts we initially offer at Mass are the bread and the wine. But we also bring to God the noblest, the most difficult, yet to God a most acceptable gift: the offering of our own selves. We offer at his altar the bread of our daily work and the wine of our suffering: in offering them to God, we surrender ourselves to die with Christ in sacrifice. This is the worship in Spirit and in Truth which the Father desires from all the baptised, in their exercise of the common priesthood of the Faithful.

This self-offering by the Faithful, symbolised by the bread and wine, only has meaning, however, in relation to the Sacrifice of Christ to which our self-offering is united. A drop of water, added to the chalice, represents the Faithful. The small drop is absorbed into the wine, just as our human nature is lost in the precious wine of Christ's divine nature. Bread and wine are offered in order that, by their consecration, they may be changed into the Sacred Body and Precious Blood of Christ, sacramentally re-presenting on the altar Christ's perfect and unique Sacrifice of love on Calvary. Thus in the Offertory Prayers of this More Ancient Roman Use, the Church concerns herself not so much with the initial offering of bread and wine, but rather anticipates what they will become: the spotless victim (*hanc immaculatam hostiam*) and the chalice of salvation (*calicem salutaris*).

The prayer accompanying the offering of bread reminds us that the Mass is not only a sacrifice of praise and thanksgiving, but that it is propitiatory: it inclines God to show his mercy in granting the forgiveness of our sins, thus reconciling us to Him. This prayer also affirms that the Mass is offered for the benefit of the Living and the Dead. The offering of the chalice is in the plural form, because in a Solemn Mass, the deacon joins the celebrant in the prayer.

The *Offerimus tibi* strongly affirms the propitiatory character of the Mass.

The prayer *In spiritu humilitatis* is reminiscent of the prayer of the three just young men, thrown into the fiery furnace (Daniel 3:39–40). The celebrant uses the plural in reciting this prayer, uniting with himself all those assembled in a common sacrifice: Christ's Faithful not only offer; they themselves are offered. Next, the *Veni, sanctificator* looks forward in a particular way to the Consecration: it is the epiclesis of this More Ancient Roman Use. The celebrant raises his hands in a circular motion as he invokes the Holy Spirit, the *Sanctificator*, the one who consecrates. The real offering in the Mass takes place at the moment of consecration and although, on the one hand, all that takes place before that moment is but a preparation, nevertheless, the Liturgy surrounds the moment of Consecration with prayers that anticipate and reiterate it, acknowledging that the transubstantiation of bread and wine into the Body and Blood of Christ is beyond the confines of space and time.

The prayers
In spiritu
humilitatis et
Veni,
Sanctificator

At a sung Mass, the incensation now occurs. The celebrant incenses the offerings firstly in a circular motion and then in the form of a Cross. Whilst performing this action he utters the simple and beautiful prayer *Incensum istud*. In the preparation of the incense, however, a prayer is recited invoking the intercession of Blessed Michael the Archangel, who is referred to as standing at the "altar of incense". Medieval writers associated Michael with the unnamed angel alluded to in Apocalypse 8:3–4.

The incensation
of the offerings

The origin of the use of incense in Christian worship owes as much to pagan Roman practices as it does to Old Testament Jewish worship. For this reason, the early Christians were suspicious of its use and some centuries passed before it became accepted and then only in processional use, rather than for the incensation of objects and persons. Consequently the principal incensations of the Mass originally accompanied processions: at the Entrance, the Gospel and the Offertory (the latter possibly derived from the Great Entrance of the Eastern Liturgies). These three occasions for the use of incense were adopted at Rome in the twelfth century. The incensation of the altar is intended as a mark of veneration for the altar as the place of sacrifice and an act of adoration and homage paid to Christ, who is symbolized by the altar. The practice is derived—ceremonially, at least—from the incensation of an altar during the rite of its consecration. Whilst incensing the altar, the celebrant recites some verses from Psalm 140. That characteristic of the More Ancient Use, wherein every ceremonial action is accompanied by a prayer, is nowhere more beautifully manifest than during the incensations at the Offertory.

The
incensation
of the altar

<table>
<tr><td>

The washing
of the hands

</td><td>

The early Christians, whose liturgy was concerned more with the utility than the symbolic meaning of rituals, nevertheless were mindful of the symbolism of the washing of the hands—purity of heart. The recitation of part of the twenty-fifth psalm—first prescribed in the Middle Ages—underlined this symbolism.

</td></tr>
</table>

The washing
of the hands

The early Christians, whose liturgy was concerned more with the utility than the symbolic meaning of rituals, nevertheless were mindful of the symbolism of the washing of the hands—purity of heart. The recitation of part of the twenty-fifth psalm—first prescribed in the Middle Ages—underlined this symbolism.

The prayer
Suscipe,
sancta Trinitas

This beautiful prayer, a summary of the things a Catholic should keep in mind when praying the Mass, is deserving of especial attention. It reminds us firstly that all our worship is offered to the One God, who is a Trinity of Persons: Father, Son and Holy Spirit. Secondly, in reflecting the Anamnesis after the consecration, the prayer insists on the unity of Christ's Paschal Mystery that is re-presented for us in sacramental form: His Passion, Resurrection and Ascension. Finally, it asserts that a secondary end of the Mass is the honour of the Saints (that is, the victory of Christ in His members is being praised), and accordingly it begs their intercession for us on Earth. Make a point of praying this prayer in the silence of your heart, uniting yourself with the words of the celebrant.

The Orate fratres
and Secret prayer

The *Orate Fratres* and the prayer which follows it, known as the Secret or Prayer over the Offerings ought to be considered together. The invitation to pray is really an extended form of the Oremus which precedes the Collect and the Postcommunion prayer. In the early Roman liturgy, when no prayers were set for the offering of the bread and wine, the Secret was prayed after the offerings were placed upon the altar. Accordingly, the Secrets are amongst the very oldest prayers of the Mass. Almost all of them express, in various ways, the notion that the presented gifts of bread and wine are instruments for the Sacrifice of Christ, rather than offerings of themselves. Secrets for feast days almost always make mention of the occasion commemorated without permitting that occasion to be the main focus of the prayer. Although the prayer is said quietly, this is not necessarily the origin of the word "secret". Opinion varies on how the word came to be attached to the prayer, since in Latin *secreta* may mean either that which is secret or that which is set apart: either being applicable to the prayer.

Preparation for the Sacrifice

Celebrant:	Dominus vobiscum.
ALL RESPOND:	**Et cum spiritu tuo.**
Celebrant:	Oremus.

The celebrant reads the Offertorium (chanted by the choir at a Sung Mass).

(THE PROPER OF THE MASS FOR THE DAY)

Then, taking the paten, he offers the bread: **SIT**

Suscipe, sancte Pater, omnipotens aeterne Deus, hanc immaculatam hostiam, quam ego indignus famulus tuus offero tibi Deo meo, vivo et vero, pro innumerabilibus peccatis, et offensionibus, et negligentiis meis, et pro omnibus circumstantibus, sed et pro omnibus fidelibus christianis vivis atque defunctis: ut mihi et illis proficiat ad salutem in vitam aeternam. Amen.

Holy Father, almighty and eternal God, receive this spotless offering which I, your unworthy servant, make to you, my living and true God, for my countless sins, offences and negligences, and for all here present, as well as for all the christian faithful, living and dead: that it may profit both them and me as a means of salvation, unto eternal life. Amen.

The celebrant pours wine and water into the chalice and blesses the water, saying:

Deus, qui humanae substantiae dignitatem mirabiliter condidisti et mirabilius reformasti: da nobis, per hujus aquae et vini mysterium, ejus divinitatis esse consortes, qui humanitatis nostrae fieri dignatus est particeps, Jesus Christus, Filius tuus, Dominus noster: Qui tecum vivit et regnat in unitate Spiritus Sancti Deus: per omnia saecula saeculorum. Amen.

O God, who in a wondrous manner formed the noble nature of man, and even more wondrously re-formed it, grant that by the mystery of this water and wine we may become partakers in his divinity, who was pleased to share our humanity: Jesus Christ your Son our Lord, who lives and reigns with you in the unity of the Holy Spirit, throughout all ages. Amen.

32

The celebrant offers the chalice, saying:

We offer to you, Lord, the chalice of salvation, entreating your mercy that for our own and the whole world's salvation, it may ascend with a sweet fragrance in the sight of your divine majesty. Amen.

Offerimus tibi, Domine, calicem salutaris, tuam deprecantes clementiam: ut in conspectu divinae majestatis tuae, pro nostra et totius mundi salute, cum odore suavitatis ascendat. Amen.

Bowing before the altar, the celebrant says:

May we be received by you, O Lord, humble in spirit and penitent in heart; and may our sacrifice be so offered in your sight this day, that it may please you, Lord God.

In spiritu humilitatis et in animo contrito suscipiamur a te, Domine: et sic fiat sacrificium nostrum in conspectu tuo hodie, ut placeat tibi, Domine Deus.

Come, O Sanctifier, almighty eternal God, and bless this sacrifice prepared for your holy name.

Veni, Sanctificator omnipotens aeterne Deus et benedic hoc sacrificium, tuo sancto nomini praeparatum.

At a Sung Mass, the celebrant prepares and blesses the incense, with which he gives honour to the offered bread and wine:

Through the intercession of blessed Michael the Archangel, who stands at the right hand of the altar of incense, and the intercession of all his chosen ones, may the Lord be pleased to bless this incense and to accept its sweet fragrance. Through Christ our Lord. Amen.

Per intercessionem beati Michaelis Archangeli, stantis a dextris altaris incensi, et omnium electorum suorum, incensum istud dignetur Dominus benedicere, et in odorem suavitatis accipere. Per Christum Dominum nostrum. Amen.

The celebrant incenses the offerings, saying:

May this incense, O Lord, which you have blessed, ascend to you, and may your mercy descend upon us.

Incensum istud a te benedictum, ascendat ad te, Domine et descendat super nos misericordia tua.

Then, the celebrant incenses the altar, saying:

Let my prayer be directed, O Lord, as incense in your sight; when I lift up my hands may it be as acceptable as the evening sacrifice. O Lord, set a guard before my mouth and a door about my lips, that my heart may not incline to evil words; to make excuses in sin.

Dirigatur, Domine, oratio mea, sicut incensum in conspectu tuo: elevatio manuum mearum sacrificium vespertinum. Pone, Domine, custodiam ori meo, et ostium circumstantiae labiis meis: ut non declinet cor meum in verba malitiae, ad excusandas excusationes in peccatis.

The celebrant hands the thurible back to the minister, saying:

Accendat in nobis Dominus ignem sui amoris, et flammam aeternae caritatis. Amen.

May the Lord kindle in us the fire of his love, and the flame of everlasting charity. Amen.

SUNG MASS

at the incensation of the people

STAND

The celebrant washes his hands, saying:

Lavabo inter innocentes manus meas et circumdabo altare tuum, Domine. Ut audiam vocem laudis et enarrem universa mirabilia tua. Domine, dilexi decorem domus tuae et locum habitationis gloriae tuae. Ne perdas cum impiis, Deus: animam meam, et cum viris sanguinum vitam meam. In quorum manibus iniquitates sunt: dextera eorum repleta est muneribus. Ego autem in innocentia mea ingressus sum: redime me, et miserere mei. Pes meus stetit in directo: in ecclesiis benedicam te, Domine. Gloria Patri, et Filio, et Spiritui Sancto. Sicut erat in principio, et nunc, et semper, et in saecula saeculorum. Amen.

I will wash my hands among the innocent and gather with them at your altar, Lord, to hear the song of praise and tell of all your wondrous works. Lord, I have loved the beauty of your house, and the place where your glory dwells. Let my soul, O God, not be lost among the wicked, nor my life with men of blood, whose hands are steeped in evil, their right hands full of bribes. But as for me, I have walked in innocence; redeem me and be merciful to me. My feet are set in the straight path; where your people gather, O Lord, I will bless you. Glory be to the Father, and to the Son, and to the Holy Spirit, as it was in the beginning, is now and ever shall be, throughout all ages. Amen.

Bowed before the altar, the celebrant prays:

Suscipe, sancta Trinitas, hanc oblationem, quam tibi offerimus ob memoriam passionis, resurrectionis, et ascensionis Jesu Christi Domini nostri: et in honorem beatae Mariae semper Virginis et beati Joannis Baptistae, et sanctorum Apostolorum Petri et Pauli, et istorum, et omnium Sanctorum: ut illis proficiat ad honorem, nobis autem ad salutem: et illi pro nobis intercedere dignentur in caelis, quorum memoriam agimus in terris. Per eundem Christum Dominum nostrum. Amen.

Accept, holy Trinity, this offering which we make to you in remembrance of the passion, resurrection and ascension of our Lord Jesus Christ, and in honour of blessed Mary ever Virgin, of blessed John the Baptist, of the holy Apostles Peter and Paul, of those whose relics rest here, and of all the Saints. To them may it bring honour, and to us salvation; and may they, whose memory we keep on earth, be pleased to intercede for us in heaven. Through the same Christ our Lord. Amen.

34

Turning to the minister, the celebrant says:

Pray brethren, that my sacrifice and yours may be acceptable to God the almighty Father.

S. May the Lord accept the sacrifice from your hands, for the praise and glory of his name, for our benefit and for that of all his holy Church.

C. Amen.

Orate, fratres: ut meum ac vestrum sacrificium acceptabile fiat apud Deum Patrem omnipotentem.

S. Suscipiat Dominus sacrificium de manibus tuis ad laudem et gloriam nominis sui, ad utilitatem quoque nostram, totiusque Ecclesiae suae sanctae.

C. Amen.

Then the celebrant prays the Secret

(THE PROPER OF THE MASS FOR THE DAY)

which he concludes with the words:

Celebrant: per omnia saecula saeculorum.

ALL RESPOND: **Amen.**

The celebrant introduces the Preface:

STAND

Celebrant: Dominus vobiscum.

ALL RESPOND: **Et cum spiritu tuo.**

Celebrant: Sursum corda.

ALL RESPOND: **Habemus ad Dominum.**

Celebrant: Gratias agamus Domine Deo nostro.

ALL RESPOND: **Dignum et justum est.**

Then he begins the Preface.

TURN TO PAGE 40

The Canon

This simple dialogue between the celebrant and the congregation, which ushers in the moment of Sacrifice, is of the greatest antiquity. The Roman priest Hippolytus uses these actual words in the *anaphora* or eucharistic prayer believed to have been written by him at the beginning of the third century. Possibly derived from the Jewish supper ritual and common to all liturgies of the East and West, it, in all likelihood, stretches back to the time of the Apostles. Whereas for the Collect and the Postcommunion, the celebrant invites all present to pray with the Greeting *Dominus vobiscum* (The Lord be with you) and the one word *Oremus* (Let us pray), at this central part of the Mass his invitation becomes three-fold. In a few words, the celebrant directs us to raise our minds and hearts to God, and to give thanks for the wonderful gift of his Son, made present in the Mass. Furthermore, by inviting those present to give thanks to God, he is requesting them to become active participants in the sacrifice which he is about to offer. Accordingly, Saint Cyprian (died 258), when discussing the Introductory Dialogue, wrote that "When we rise to pray, we must be careful to give our attention whole-heartedly to the prayers we say. Every thought of the world or worldly things must retire into the background, so that the soul may contemplate nothing but the content of the prayer."

The Introductory Dialogue

Truly, it is fitting and just, says the celebrant, continuing the sentiments of the congregation's *Dignum et justum est*, and making explicit that the *Preface* is a hymn of praise and thanksgiving. It is well to remember that the Sacrifice of the Mass is the supreme act of worship in which the Church on earth, together with those in Purgatory and the Angels and Saints join in praise and thanksgiving to the All-holy God, through the mediation of Christ. The Sacrifice is his and he permits us to associate ourselves with it. With great reverence, we should foster that disposition of heart which underlies the Preface, praising with gratitude God the Creator, God the Saviour, God the Author of the mystery that is being celebrated. The sublime words of the Preface, which alter according to the Season or Feast, bear much consideration, expressing as they do a particular mystery of our Faith in the most admirable but concise fashion. The conclusion of each Preface makes reference to the praise of the whole Company of Heaven, which continues without ceasing. At this dramatic moment, the unity of the Church on earth and all in Heaven is demonstrated most solemnly and we are permitted to enter into the heavenly choir and to join our voices with theirs in their song of joy in honour of the Blessed Trinity. The *Sanctus* is derived from Isaiah 6:3 and is believed to have been incorporated into the Mass at a very early date: Pope Saint Clement I (died 101) quotes it in his letter to the Corinthians. It is a hymn common to all liturgies of the East and West.

The Preface and Sanctus

The *Canon* of the Mass, so called from the Greek word for "rule" reached its present form by the sixth century, although most of it is very much older. It is believed to have been edited in the fourth century, using various other existing eucharistic prayers as a model, by one man (probably Ambrose, bishop of Milan). Before the Canon had been set down, it had been the practice of the celebrant to improvise his own prayer, which he sang aloud. Whereas in some places the great mystery of the Consecration was originally hidden from the gaze of the congregation by a curtain drawn before the altar, by the ninth century it came to be the practice instead to pray the Canon silently. And so, when the Sanctus is concluded a stillness of reverential awe ensues. The celebrant now enters into the "Holy of Holies" lifting up his eyes, hands and hearts to heaven, beseeching God's help for what he is about to do in the person of Christ, and thereafter he bows low again before the altar in acknowledgement of his unworthiness. All human means are as nothing at Christ's coming amongst us under the lowly appearances of bread and wine in the hands of the celebrant.

The difference between the primitive Eucharist prayers and the Roman Canon is most evident in the intercessory elements which, from the fourth century onward, crept into the Canon. At around the same time that the *Prayer of the Faithful* ceased to be read at Mass, the *Mementos* entered the Canon. The celebrant prays that the fruits of the Sacrifice of the Mass may benefit those who offer it. Firstly, he recalls the *Church on earth*, the Pope, the bishop and all who faithfully teach and preach the Gospel. Secondly, the *living*. The celebrant joins his hands and recalls the names of the persons for whom he may be offering the Mass, and we, with him, remember those who are especially near to us; our relations and all those who are present at Mass.

The commemoration of the living is connected with the *Saints*, because when we offer the Sacrifice of the Mass, we are in communion with all those in Heaven, with whom we prayed the Sanctus and whose glory is solely attributable to the Sacrifice of their Redemption. It is not just a recollection, though: we venerate the Elect in Heaven and ask for their intercession. Pre-eminently, we venerate and invoke the intercession of the Blessed Virgin Mary. Then, some of the Apostles—Peter to Thaddæus (Jude)—are named, followed by several early Popes, Linus to Cornelius, then Cyprian, bishop of Carthage and several other Roman martyrs. The fact that only Roman martyrs are included has no greater significance than that this prayer was written for use in Rome and at a time when the persecution of Christians in that city was hardly finished.

Saying this prayer, the celebrant holds his hands extended over the offerings. This is the the the earliest form of Blessing, before the practice of making the sign of the Cross over an object had arisen. Pius Parsch (*The Liturgy of the Mass*, p. 236) writes that at the sacrifice of Atonement the Jewish priests would extend their hands over the victim to transfer symbolically the guilt of their own sins to the animal victim, which was then burnt. But in the New Law, this gesture is transformed. The Christian priest signifies that Christ, in dying on the Cross —the perfect sacrifice which replaced the old law—really takes upon himself the sins of all mankind.

The
Hanc igitur

The words which recount Christ's institution of the Blessed Eucharist are the most ancient words of the Mass and represent a tradition which pre-dates the writing of the New Testament. Almost all the formulae of Consecration in the Eastern and Western Liturgies are fundamentally the same and substantially agree with the words set down in the Gospels and in Saint Paul's first Epistle to the Corinthians. From such historical evidence and from what has been handed down from one century to the next, we can be certain of the words uttered by Christ at the Last Supper and, moreover, what the Apostles understood by them. Over the centuries, as the understanding of the nature of the Mass became more developed theologically, the Church invested the moment of Consecration with more and more ceremony. Originally, for example, there were no genuflections after the Consecration, because the genuflection was a pagan mark of respect for authority. Furthermore, the most striking part of the Consecration ceremonies, the Elevation, was introduced into the Mass in the eleventh century when theological speculation arose about the Real Presence of Christ in the Eucharist. Not surprisingly, both genuflections and elevations were excluded from Protestant services devised at the time of the Reformation. The celebrant, mindful that what he is uttering is not merely an historical recollection of the Last Supper, but the formula by which Christ becomes really and substantially present under the appearance of bread and wine, strives to intrude as little as possible of his own personality into the words, but follows strictly the Rule or *Canon*. For at this moment, Christ is the priest of the sacrifice and his human representative retires into insignificance. Christ is the celebrant; the priest merely his visible instrument, so that now his actions and words become identical with those of Christ at the Last Supper.

The Consecration

The Anamnesis	This very ancient prayer, in all likelihood going back to apostolic times, is known in Greek as the *anamnesis* because it states that the Church acts in memory of our Lord and in accordance with his command, "Whenever you shall do these things, you shall do them for my Commemoration." The Anamnesis stresses the unity of the Paschal Mystery which is sacramentally represented on the altar: the Passion, Death, Resurrection and Ascension of the Lord. This prayer and the *Supplices te rogamus* set before God the Sacrifice effected on the altar. The wording of this prayer aptly expresses the people's participation with the celebrant in offering the Holy Sacrifice.
The Supra quae propitio and Supplices	The Old Testament sacrifices of Abel, Abraham and Melchisedech are prefigurations of the Sacrifice of Christ and of the Mass: in the Scripture and the writings of the Church Fathers, these three men are taken as types of our Lord. In the *supplices te rogamus*, the "altar on high" is the one referred to at Apocalypse 8:3–4, the golden altar which is before the throne of God and where an angel stands to offer the prayers of the Church with incense. Whilst the Church on earth celebrates the Sacred Liturgy, a celestial Liturgy is offered by the saints in heaven, and from the union of these two sacrificial Liturgies, we pray that the fruits of the sacrifice may be given to us. When the celebrant utters this prayer, his ceremonial actions emphasise what is being said: he bows low at the word *Supplices* (suppliants), kisses the altar, then makes the sign of the Cross over the offerings and lastly upon himself.
The Memento of the dead	The Church Fathers taught that prayers for the dead when offered during the Mass are especially salutory. St. Augustine in his letter *Concerning our duties towards the dead*, commented on the consolation we derive from the thought that the Church during the Holy Sacrifice remembers all those who have died in Christ, so that even those who have neither parents, nor children, nor friends, nor relations left to pray for them when they are dead, can at least count on the prayers of one mother—the Church.
Nobis quoque peccatoribus	The first three words of this prayer are uttered aloud by the celebrant, originally partly to indicate that the Canon was drawing to a close, and also to invite the other clergy present in the sanctuary to recall their unworthiness and beseech the Divine assistance. But the prayer is also the opportunity for all present to pray for themselves. The Church, the Living and the Dead have all previously been remembered, but this Memento is for those assembled. This prayer is animated by that same spirit of humility which inspired the conclusion of the Preface. The

celebrant strikes his breast as he begins this prayer, reminiscent of the publican described at Luke 18:9–14 who entered the Temple to pray, striking his breast and saying "O God, be merciful to me, a sinner." Again we are reminded that we join with the Communion of Saints in offering our worship to God and although we are unworthy to be numbered in the fellowship of the saints, we ask for this fellowship not because of our own merit, but entirely relying on God's goodness and mercy. A list of martyrs, balancing the list given in the first half of the Canon is then given. First, John the Baptist; then Stephen, the deacon; then two who were numbered amongst the Apostles in the early Church, Matthias and Barnabas, followed by Ignatius the bishop of Antioch, Alexander, and two who were martyred together, Marcellinus and Peter. Then six women martyrs, all of whom were especially venerated at Rome.

The Canon closes with the great doxology to the Holy Trinity, the words of which are adapted from Saint Paul (Romans 11:36): no other doxology is invested with such solemnity. Before the eleventh century, this was the only elevation in the Mass, although its importance has been somewhat overshadowed by the Elevations after the Consecration. The glorification of God is the final purpose of the whole of Christ's redemptive work: to restore to God that glory of which he had been deprived by mankind's sin. Accordingly, the Mass, which makes Redemption present and actual to us, can have no other purpose but this. The concluding words *Per omnia saecula saeculorum* are chanted or recited aloud by the celebrant, a survival of the time when the entire Canon was prayed aloud. When we respond *Amen*, we join with Christ and the entire Church in worshipping God: it is our identification with what has been done. Since the earliest days of the Church, Christians have uttered this single word to conclude the Canon.

The Doxology

The Preface

Then he begins the Preface.

Preface of the Most Holy Trinity

The Preface of the Holy Trinity is used on the Feast of the Most Holy Trinity and on the Sundays before Lent and after Pentecost.

STAND

It is truly fitting and just, right and profitable for our salvation, always and everywhere to give thanks to you, Lord, holy Father, almighty, eternal God. With your only-begotten Son and the Holy Spirit, you are one God, one Lord, not in the singleness of one Person, but in a Trinity of one substance. For, whatever we believe through your revelation about your glory, the same also we believe about your Son and about the Holy Spirit, without distinction or difference. So that in acknowledging the true and eternal Godhead, we adore each individual person, and at the same time, their one substance and their equal majesty: which the Angels, the Archangels, the Cherubim and the Seraphim all praise, never ceasing to cry out with one voice:

Vere dignum et justum est, aequum et salutare nos tibi semper, et ubique gratias agere: Domine, sancte Pater omnipotens aeterne Deus. Qui cum unigenito Filio tuo, et Spiritu Sancto, unus es Deus, unus es Dominus: non in unius singularitate personae, sed in unius Trinitate substantiae. Quod enim de tua gloria, revelante te, credimus, hoc de Filio tuo, hoc de Spiritu Sancto, sine differentia discretionis sentimus. Ut in confessione verae, sempiternaeque Deitatis, et in personis proprietas, et in essentia unitas, et in majestate adoretur aequalitas. Quam laudant Angeli atque Archangeli, Cherubim quoque ac Seraphim: qui non cessant clamare quotidie, una voce dicentes:

Then all say together, or sing with the choir:

Sanctus, Sanctus, Sanctus,
Dominus Deus Sabaoth.
Pleni sunt caeli et terra gloria tua,
Hosanna in excelsis.
✠ Benedictus qui venit in nomine Domini.
Hosanna in excelsis.

TURN TO PAGE 51

The following prefaces are used according to the season or feast:

Preface of Advent	Preface of the Blessed Sacrament
Preface of Christmas	Preface of the Sacred Heart
Preface of the Epiphany	Preface of the Blessed Virgin Mary
Preface of Lent	Preface of the Apostles
Preface of the Holy Cross	Preface of All Saints
Preface of the Lord's Supper	Preface of Christ the King
Preface of Easter	Preface of Saint Joseph
Preface of the Ascension	Common Preface
Preface of the Holy Spirit	Preface of the Dedication of a Church
	Preface of the Dead

Preface of Advent

Vere dignum et justum est, aequum et salutare, nos tibi semper, et ubique gratias agere: Domine, sancte Pater omnipotens aeterne Deus: per Christum Dominum nostrum. Quem perdito hominum generi Salvatorem misericors et fidelis promisisti: cujus veritas instrueret inscios, sanctitas justificaret impios, virtus adjuvaret infirmos. Dum ergo prope est ut veniat quem missurus es, et dies affulget liberationis nostrae, in hac promissionum tuarum fide, piis gaudiis exsultamus. Et ideo cum Angelis et Archangelis, cum Thronis et Dominationibus, cumque omni militia caelestis exercitus, hymnum gloriae tuae canimus, sine fine dicentes: **Sanctus...**

It is truly fitting and just, right and profitable for our salvation, always and everywhere to give thanks to you, Lord, holy Father, almighty, eternal God, through Christ our Lord, whom you, the merciful and faithful, promised as Saviour for the lost race of mankind; a Saviour whose truth would teach the unknowing, whose holiness would make righteous the wicked and whose virtue would assist the weak. Now, the time for the Coming of him whom you are going to send is at hand, and the day of our liberation shines forth. And so, with the Angels and Archangels, with the Thrones and Dominations, and all the strength of the heavenly host, rejoicing with holy gladness and trusting in your promises, we sing without ceasing this hymn to your glory: Turn to p. 51

Preface of Christmas

Vere dignum et justum est, aequum et salutare, nos tibi semper, et ubique gratias agere: Domine, sancte Pater omnipotens aeterne Deus: Quia per incarnati Verbi mysterium, nova mentis nostrae oculis lux tuae claritatis infulsit: ut dum visibiliter Deum cognoscimus, per hunc in invisibilium amorem rapiamur. Et ideo cum Angelis et Archangelis, cum Thronis et Dominationibus, cumque omni militia caelestis exercitus, hymnum gloriae tuae canimus, sine fine dicentes: **Sanctus...**

It is truly fitting and just, right and profitable for our salvation, always and everywhere to give thanks to you, Lord, holy Father, almighty, eternal God, because through the mystery of the Word made flesh a new light of your glory has shone upon the eyes of our mind, so that as we come to know God in visible form, we may be drawn through him to the love of things beyond our seeing. And so, with the Angels and Archangels, with the Thrones and Dominations, and all the strength of the heavenly host, we sing without ceasing this hymn to your glory: Turn to p. 51

Preface of the Epiphany

Vere dignum et justum est, aequum et salutare, nos tibi semper, et ubique gratias agere: Domine, sancte Pater omnipotens aeterne Deus: Quia, cum Unigenitus tuus in substantia nostrae mortalitatis apparuit, nova nos immortalitatis

It is truly fitting and just, right and profitable for our salvation, always and everywhere to give thanks to you, Lord, holy Father, almighty, eternal God, because when your only-begotten Son appeared in the substance of our human nature, he restored us by the new radiance of

42

his immortalilty. And so, with the Angels and Archangels, with the Thrones and Dominations, and all the strength of the heavenly host, we sing without ceasing this hymn to your glory:

Turn to p. 51

suae luce reparavit. Et ideo cum Angelis et Archangelis, cum Thronis et Dominationibus, cumque omni militia caelestis exercitus, hymnum gloriae tuae canimus, sine fine dicentes: **Sanctus...**

Preface of Lent

It is truly fitting and just, right and profitable for our salvation, always and everywhere to give thanks to you, Lord, holy Father, almighty, eternal God. By our fasting you temper our defects, raise up our minds and give us virtue, with its reward, through Christ our Lord, through whom the Angels praise your majesty, the Dominations adore, the Powers stand in awe. The Heavens and the heavenly Hosts together with the blessed Seraphim, in exultant chorus unite to celebrate it. Grant, we implore you, that our voices also may be joined with theirs, to say with lowly praise: Turn to p. 51

Vere dignum et justum est, aequum et salutare, nos tibi semper, et ubique gratias agere: Domine, sancte Pater omnipotens aeterne Deus: Qui corporali jejunio vitia comprimis, mentem elevas, virtutem largiris, et praemia: per Christum Dominum nostrum. Per quem majestatem tuam laudant Angeli, adorant Dominationes, tremunt Potestates. Caeli, caelorumque Virtutes, ac beata Seraphim, socia exsultatione concelebrant. Cum quibus et nostras voces, ut admitti jubeas, deprecamur, supplici confessione dicentes: **Sanctus...**

Preface of the Holy Cross

It is truly fitting and just, right and profitable for our salvation, always and everywhere to give thanks to you, Lord, holy Father, almighty, eternal God. You established the salvation of the human race on the wood of the Cross, so that, whence death appeared, from there life might spring again and in order that Satan, who conquered by a tree, might also be conquered by a tree, through Christ our Lord, through whom the Angels praise your majesty, the Dominations adore, the Powers stand in awe. The Heavens and the heavenly Hosts together with the blessed Seraphim, in exultant chorus unite to celebrate it. Grant, we implore you, that our voices also may be joined with theirs, to say with lowly praise: Turn to p. 51

Vere dignum et justum est, aequum et salutare, nos tibi semper, et ubique gratias agere: Domine, sancte Pater omnipotens aeterne Deus: Qui salutem humani generis in ligno Crucis constituisti: ut unde mors oriebatur, inde vita resurgeret: et qui in ligno vincebat, in ligno quoque vinceretur: per Christum Dominum nostrum. Per quem majestatem tuam laudant Angeli, adorant Dominationes, tremunt Potestates. Caeli, caelorumque Virtutes, ac beata Seraphim, socia exsultatione concelebrant. Cum quibus et nostras voces, ut admitti jubeas, deprecamur, supplici confessione dicentes: **Sanctus...**

Preface of the Mass of the Lord's Supper

Vere dignum et justum est, aequum et salutare, nos tibi semper, et ubique gratias agere: Domine, sancte Pater omnipotens aeterne Deus: per Christum Dominum nostrum, verum aeternumque Pontificem, et solum sine peccatimacula Sacerdotem. Qui in novissima Cena formam sacrificii perennis instituens, hostiam se tibi primum obtulit, et primus docuit offerri. Cujus carne pro nobis immolata dum pascimur, roboramur, et fuso sanguine dum potamur, abluimur. Et ideo cum Angelis et Archangelis, cum Thronis et Dominationibus, cumque omni militia caelestis exercitus, hymnum gloriae tuae canimus, sine fine dicentes: **Sanctus ...**

It is truly fitting and just, right and profitable for our salvation, always and everywhere to give thanks to you, Lord, holy Father, almighty, eternal God, through Christ our Lord, the true and eternal High Priest and, alone, the Priest without stain of sin. In the Last Supper, establishing the form of the eternal sacrifice, he firstly offered himself to you as a victim, thus teaching us the noblest and best offering. By his body, sacrificed for us, we are now fed, we are now strengthened; by his poured-out blood we are now given drink, we are now cleansed. And so, with the Angels and Archangels, with the Thrones and Dominations, and all the strength of the heavenly host, we sing without ceasing this hymn to your glory: Turn to p. 51

Preface of Easter

Vere dignum et justum est, aequum et salutare: Te quidem, Domine, omni tempore, sed in hoc potissimum [in hac potissimum die] gloriosius praedicare, cum Pascha nostrum immolatus est Christus. Ipse enim verus est Agnus, qui abstulit peccata mundi. Qui mortem nostram moriendo destruxit, et vitam resurgendo reparavit. Et ideo cum Angelis et Archangelis, cum Thronis et Dominationibus, cumque omni militia caelestis exercitus, hymnum gloriae tuae canimus, sine fine dicentes: **Sanctus ...**

It is truly fitting and just, right and profitable for our salvation to proclaim your glory at all times, but more especially in this season [*on this day*], when Christ our Pasch was sacrificed. For he is the true Lamb who has taken away the sins of the world; who by dying, destroyed our death and by rising restored life. And so, with the Angels and Archangels, with the Thrones and Dominations, and all the strength of the heavenly host, we sing without ceasing this hymn to your glory: Turn to p. 51

Preface of the Ascension

Vere dignum et justum est, aequum et salutare, nos tibi semper, et ubique gratias agere: Domine, sancte Pater omnipotens aeterne Deus: per Christum Dominum nostrum. Qui post resurrectionem suam omnibus discipulis suis manifestus apparuit,

It is truly fitting and just, right and profitable for our salvation, always and everywhere to give thanks to you, Lord, holy Father, almighty, eternal God, through Christ our Lord, who, after his resurrection appeared visibly to all his disciples and, while they watched, was lifted

44

up into heaven, in order to make us sharers in his divinity. And so, with the Angels and Archangels, with the Thrones and Dominations, and all the strength of the heavenly host, we sing without ceasing this hymn to your glory:

Turn to p. 51

et ipsis cernentibus est elevatus in caelum, ut nos divinitatis suae tribueret esse particeps. Et ideo cum Angelis et Archangelis, cum Thronis et Dominationibus, cumque omni militia caelestis exercitus, hymnum gloriae tuae canimus, sine fine dicentes: **Sanctus...**

Preface of the Holy Spirit

It is truly fitting and just, right and profitable for our salvation, always and everywhere to give thanks to you, Lord, holy Father, almighty, eternal God, through Christ our Lord, who, having ascended above all the heavens and having taken his seat at your right hand, poured forth [this day] the Holy Spirit upon his adopted sons, according to his promise. Accordingly, the whole world rejoices with unbounded joy. The heavenly hosts also, and the angelic powers join in a hymn to your glory, crying out unceasingly: Turn to p. 51

Vere dignum et justum est, aequum et salutare, nos tibi semper, et ubique gratias agere: Domine, sancte Pater omnipotens aeterne Deus: per Christum Dominum nostrum. Qui ascendens super omnes caelos, sedensque ad dexteram tuam, promissum Spiritum Sanctum [hodierna die] in filios adoptionis effudit. Quapropter profusis gaudiis, totus in orbe terrarum mundus exsultat. Sed et supernae Virtutes, atque angelicae Potestates, hymnum gloriae tuae concinunt, sine fine dicentes: **Sanctus...**

Preface of the Blessed Sacrament

It is truly fitting and just, right and profitable for our salvation, always and everywhere to give thanks to you, Lord, holy Father, almighty, eternal God, through Christ our Lord, who, having set aside the empty signs of animal victims, commemorated his Body and Blood for us in sacrifice, in order that the pure oblation which alone was acceptable to you, may be offered to your name in every place. Therefore, in the mystery of his unsearchable wisdom and unbounded love, that which once he accomplished completely on the Cross, he does not cease miraculously to produce, he himself offering it and he himself the offering. And, having become a single offering with him, he invites us to the sacred banquet in which he himself is received as food, in which the memory of his Passion is recalled, the soul filled with

Vere dignum et justum est, aequum et salutare, nos tibi semper, et ubique gratias agere: Domine, sancte Pater omnipotens aeterne Deus: per Christum Dominum nostrum. Qui, remotis carnalium victimarum inanibus umbris, Corpus et Sanguinem suum nobis in sacrificium commendavit: ut in omni loco offeratur nomini tuo, quae tibi sola complacuit, oblatio munda. In hoc igitur inscrutabilis sapientiae, et immensae caritatis mysterio, idipsum quod semel in Cruce perfecit, non cessat mirabiliter operari, ipse offerens, ipse et oblatio. Et nos, unam secum hostiam effectos, ad sacrum invitat convivium, in quo ipse cibus noster sumitur, recolitur memoria Passionis ejus, mens impletur gratia, et futurae nobis pignus datur. Et ideo cum Angelis et Archangelis, cum Thronis et Dominationibus, cumque omni militia caelestis exercitus, hymnum gloriae tuae canimus, sine fine dicentes: **Sanctus...**

grace and a foretaste of the future is to us given. And so, with the Angels and Archangels, with the Thrones and Dominations, and all the strength of the heavenly host, we sing without ceasing this hymn to your glory: Turn to p. 51

Preface of the Sacred Heart

Vere dignum et justum est, aequum et salutare, nos tibi semper, et ubique gratias agere: Domine, sancte Pater omnipotens aeterne Deus: Qui Unigenitum tuum in cruce pendentem lanceae militis transfigi voluisti, ut apertum Cor, divinae largitatis sacrarium, torrentes nobis funderet miserationis et gratiae, et quod amore nostri flagrare numquam destitit, piis esset requies et poenitentibus pateret salutis refugium. Et ideo cum Angelis et Archangelis, cum Thronis et Dominationibus, cumque omni militia caelestis exercitus, hymnum gloriae tuae canimus, sine fine dicentes: **Sanctus...**

It is truly fitting and just, right and profitable for our salvation, always and everywhere to give thanks to you, Lord, holy Father, almighty, eternal God, who desired that your Only-begotten Son should be lanced by a soldier's spear as he hung upon the Cross, so that from his pierced heart a stream of mercy and grace might be poured out upon us, as from a treasury of divine goodness, and so that in his heart, ever-burning with love for us, the devout may find a place of rest and the repentant a refuge of salvation. And so, with the Angels and Archangels, with the Thrones and Dominations, and all the strength of the heavenly host, we sing without ceasing this hymn to your glory: Turn to p. 51

Preface of the Blessed Virgin Mary

Vere dignum et justum est, aequum et salutare, nos tibi semper, et ubique gratias agere: Domine, sancte Pater omnipotens aeterne Deus: Et te in festivitate beatae Mariae semper Virginis collaudare, benedicere et praedicare. Quae et Unigenitum tuum Sancti Spiritus obumbratione concepit: et virginitatis gloria permanente, lumen aeternum mundo effudit, Jesum Christum Dominum nostrum. Per quem majestatem tuam laudant Angeli, adorant Dominationes, tremunt Potestates. Caeli, caelorumque Virtutes, ac beata Seraphim, socia exsultatione concelebrant. Cum quibus et nostras voces, ut admitti jubeas, deprecamur, supplici confessione dicentes: **Sanctus...**

It is truly fitting and just, right and profitable for our salvation, always and everywhere to give thanks to you, Lord, holy Father, almighty, eternal God, and to praise, bless and proclaim you on this feast of the Blessed Virgin Mary who, by the overshadowing of the Holy Spirit, and whilst preserving her glorious virginity, gave forth to the world the eternal light, Jesus Christ our Lord, through whom the Angels praise your majesty, the Dominations adore, the Powers stand in awe. The Heavens and the heavenly Hosts together with the blessed Seraphim, in exultant chorus unite to celebrate it. Grant, we implore you, that our voices also may be joined with theirs, to say with lowly praise: Turn to p. 51

Preface of the Apostles

It is truly fitting and just, right and profitable for our salvation humbly to implore you, Lord, not to abandon the flock of which you are eternal shepherd, but to guard it with continual protection through your blessed Apostles, so that your flock may be governed by those guides, whom as vicars of your work you have appointed to rule as shepherds. And so, with the Angels and Archangels, with the Thrones and Dominations, and all the strength of the heavenly host, we sing without ceasing this hymn to your glory: Turn to p. 51

Vere dignum et justum est, aequum et salutare: Te, Domine, suppliciter exorare, ut gregem tuum, pastor aeterne, non deseras: sed per beatos Apostolos tuos, continua protectione custodias: ut iisdem rectoribus gubernetur, quos operis tui vicarios eidem contulisti praeesse pastores. Et ideo cum Angelis et Archangelis, cum Thronis et Dominationibus, cumque omni militia caelestis exercitus, hymnum gloriae tuae canimus, sine fine dicentes: **Sanctus...**

Preface of All Saints and the Holy Patrons

It is truly fitting and just, right and profitable for our salvation, always and everywhere to give thanks to you, Lord, holy Father, almighty, eternal God, Glorified by the company of saints, you crown your own gifts by crowning their good works. In their conduct, you give an example to us; in their communion, a fellowship and in their intercession, a help, so that, having such a multitude of witnesses set over us, we may, through endurance, hasten towards our intended struggle and attain with them the imperishable crown of glory, through Jesus Christ our Lord, by whose blood, the entrance to the eternal kingdom is purveyed, and through whom the Angels, atremble, together with the entire company of heaven, united in exultant chorus, adore your majesty. Grant, we humbly pray you, that our voices may be joined with theirs, to say with lowly praise: Turn to p. 51

Vere dignum et justum est, aequuum et salutare, nos tibi semper, et ubique gratias agere: Domine, sancte Pater omnipotens aeterne Deus; qui glorificaris in concilio Sanctorum, et eorum coronando merita, coronas dona tua: qui nobis in eorum praebes, et conversatione exemplum, et communione consortium, et intercessione subsidium: ut tantam habentes impositam nubem testium, per patientiam curramus ad propositum nobis certamen, et cum eis percipiamus immarcescibilem gloriae coronam. Per Jesum Christum Dominum nostrum, cujus sanguine ministratur nobis introitus in aeternum regnum. Per quem majestatem tuam trementes adorant Angeli, et omnes spiritum caelestium chori socia exsulatione concelebrant. Cum quibus et nostras voces, ut admitti jubeas, deprecamur, supplici confessione dicentes: **Sanctus...**

Preface of Christ the King

Vere dignum et justum est, aequum et salutare, nos tibi semper, et ubique gratias agere: Domine, sancte Pater omnipotens aeterne Deus: Qui Unigenitum Filium tuum Dominum nostrum Jesum Christum, Sacerdotem aeternum et universorum Regem, oleo exsultationis unxisti: ut, seipsum in ara crucis, hostiam immaculatam et pacificam offerens, redemptionis humanae sacramenta perageret: et suo subjectis imperio omnibus creaturis, aeternum et universale regnum immensae tuae traderet Majestati: regnum veritas et vitae; regnum sanctitatis et gratiae; regnum justitiae, amoris et pacis. Et ideo cum Angelis et Archangelis, cum Thronis et Dominationibus, cumque omni militia caelestis exercitus, hymnum gloriae tuae canimus, sine fine dicentes: **Sanctus...**

It is truly fitting and just, right and profitable for our salvation, always and everywhere to give thanks to you, Lord, holy Father, almighty, eternal God, who anointed your only-begotten Son, our Lord Jesus Christ, with the oil of gladness to be the eternal Priest and King of the Universe, so that by giving himself as an unblemished victim for peace upon the altar of the Cross, he might accomplish the rite of man's redemption and, having made the entire creation subject to his rule, might hand over to your infinite Majesty an eternal and universal kingdom: a kingdom of truth and life, a kingdom of holiness and grace, a kingdom of justice, love and peace. And so, with the Angels and Archangels, with the Thrones and Dominations, and all the strength of the heavenly host, we sing without ceasing this hymn to your glory: Turn to p. 51

Preface of Saint Joseph

Vere dignum et justum est, aequum et salutare, nos tibi semper, et ubique gratias agere: Domine, sancte Pater omnipotens aeterne Deus. Et te in festivitate [solemnitate] beati Joseph debitis magnificare praeconiis, benedicere et praedicare. Qui et vir justus, a te Deiparae Virgini Sponsus est datus: et fidelis servus ac prudens, super familiam tuam in constitutus: ut Unigenitum tuum Sancti Spiritus obumbratione conceptum, paterna vice custodiret, Jesum Christum Dominum nostrum. Per quem majestatem tuam laudant Angeli, adorant Dominationes, tremunt Potestates. Caeli caelorumque Virtutes, ac beata Seraphim, socia exsulatione concelebrant. Cum quibus et nostras voces, ut admitti jubeas, deprecamur, supplici confessione dicentes: **Sanctus...**

It is truly fitting and just, right and profitable for our salvation, always and everywhere to give thanks to you, Lord, holy Father, almighty, eternal God, and fitting that we should glorify, bless and confess your name with due praise on this feast [*or Solemnity*] of blessed Joseph, the just man whom you gave as Husband to the Virgin Mother of God. He was the faithful and prudent servant whom you set over your family to be guardian and foster-father of your Only-begotten Son, our Lord Jesus Christ, who was conceived by the overshadowing of the Holy Spirit and through whom the Angels praise your majesty, the Dominations adore, the Powers stand in awe. The Heavens and the heavenly Hosts together with the blessed Seraphim, in exultant chorus unite to celebrate it. Grant, we implore you, that our voices also may be joined with theirs, to say with lowly praise: Turn to p. 51

Common Preface

It is truly fitting and just, right and profitable for our salvation, always and everywhere to give thanks to you, Lord, holy Father, almighty, eternal God, through Christ our Lord, through whom the Angels praise your majesty, the Dominations adore, the Powers stand in awe. The Heavens and the heavenly Hosts together with the blessed Seraphim, in exultant chorus unite to celebrate it. Grant, we implore you, that our voices also may be joined with theirs, to say with lowly praise: Turn to p. 51

Vere dignum et justum est, aequum et salutare, nos tibi semper, et ubique gratias agere: Domine, sancte Pater omnipotens aeterne Deus: per Christum Dominum nostrum. Per quem majestatem tuam laudant Angeli, adorant Dominationes, tremunt Potestates. Caeli, caelorumque Virtutes, ac beata Seraphim, socia exsultatione concelebrant. Cum quibus et nostras voces, ut admitti jubeas, deprecamur, supplici confessione dicentes: **Sanctus...**

Preface of the Dedication of a Church

It is truly fitting and just, right and profitable for our salvation, always and everywhere to give thanks to you, Lord, holy Father, almighty, eternal God: the giver of all good gifts, who dwells in this house of prayer (which we have built), and unceasingly sanctifies the Church which you founded. For your Church is the true house of prayer signified by these visible buildings, the temple where your glory dwells, the seat of unchanging truth, the sanctuary of eternal charity. She is the ark which rescues us from the floodwaters of this world and brings us into the port of salvation. She is the one beloved Bride whom Christ acquired by his blood and gives life by his Holy Spirit. In her bosom we are born anew by your grace, nourished by the milk of your word, strengthened by the bread of life, continually sustained by your merciful assistance. With the help of her Bridegroom, she struggles faithfully on earth and, crowned by him, triumphs. And so, with the Angels and Archangels, with the Thrones and Dominations, and all the strength of the heavenly host, we sing without ceasing this hymn to your glory: Turn to p. 51

Vere dignum et justum est, aequum et salutare, nos tibi semper et ubique gratias agere: Domine, sancte Pater, omnipotens aeterne Deus: Qui hanc orationis domum (quam aedificavimus), bonorum omnium largitor inhabitas, et Ecclesiam, quam ipse fundasti, incessabili operatione sanctificas. Haec est enim vere domum orationis, visibilibus aedificiis adumbrata, templum habitationis gloriae tuae, sedes incommutabilis veritatis, sanctuarium aeternae caritatis. Haec est arca, quae nos a mundi ereptos diluvio, in portum salutis inducit. Haec est dilecta et unica sponsa, quam acquisivit Christus sanguine suo, cujus in sinu renati per gratiam tuam, lacte verbi pascimur, pane vitae roboramur, misericordiae tuae subsidiis confovemur. Haec fideliter in terris Sponso adjuvante, militat, et perenniter in caelis, ipso coronante, triumphat. Et ideo cum Angelis et Archangelis, cum Thronis et Dominationibus, cumque omni militia caelestis exercitus, hymnum gloriae tuae canimus, sine fine dicentes: **Sanctus...**

Preface of the Dead

Vere dignum et justum est, aequum et salutare, nos tibi semper, et ubique gratias agere: Domine, sancte Pater omnipotens aeterne Deus: per Christum Dominum nostrum. In quo nobis spes beatae resurrectionis effulsit, ut quos contristat certa moriendi conditio, eosdem consoletur futurae immortalitatis promissio. Tuis enim fidelibus, Domine, vita mutatur, non tollitur, et dissoluta terrestris hujus incolatus domo, aeterna in caelis habitatio comparatur. Et ideo cum Angelis et Archangelis, cum Thronis et Dominationibus, cumque omni militia caelestis exercitus, hymnum gloriae tuae canimus, sine fine dicentes:
Sanctus ...

It is truly fitting and just, right and profitable for our salvation, always and everywhere to give thanks to you, Lord, holy Father, almighty, eternal God, through Christ our Lord, in whom the hope of a blessed resurrection has shone forth, comforting with the promise of future immortality those who are saddened by the human condition's fate of death. For your faithful people, O Lord, life is changed, not taken away; for, when the place of this earthly dwelling is dissolved in death, an eternal home is prepared in heaven. And so, with the Angels and Archangels, with the Thrones and Dominations, and all the strength of the heavenly host, we sing without ceasing this hymn to your glory: Turn to p. 51

AFTER THE SANCTUS, KNEEL

Then the celebrant, bowed, recites the Sanctus;
at a Sung Mass, the congregation joins the choir in chanting the Sanctus:

Sanctus, sanctus, sanctus, Dominus Deus Sabaoth.
Pleni sunt caeli et terra gloria tua.
Hosanna in excelsis.
✠ **Benedictus qui venit in nomine Domini.**
Hosanna in excelsis.

Holy, holy, holy is the Lord God of Mighty Hosts.
The heavens and earth are filled with your glory
Hosanna in the highest.
✠ Blessed is he who comes in the Lord's name.
Hosanna in the highest.

At the Sanctus

THE CANON

The celebrant kisses the altar and, bowing profoundly, he prays quietly:

TE igitur clementissime Pater, per Jesum Christum Filium tuum, Dominum nostrum, supplices rogamus, ac petimus, uti accepta habeas, et benedicas, haec ✠ dona, haec ✠ munera, haec sancta ✠ sacrificia illibata, in primis, quae tibi offerimus pro Ecclesia tua sancta catholica: quam pacificare, custodire, adunare, et regere digneris toto orbe terrarum: una cum famulo tuo Papa nostro N et Antistite nostro N et omnibus orthodoxis, atque catholicae et apostolicae fidei cultoribus.

O Father most merciful, in humble prayer we approach you; praying to you for the love of your Son, our Lord Jesus Christ, that this gift of ours, this tribute of ours, this sacrifice holy and unblemished, will be welcomed with your blessing. And above all else, for your holy Church universal we offer it: peace and unity grant her, your guardianship and guidance all the world over. On all alike have mercy, on N our Pope and N our bishop, and all who reverence the right-teaching of the Catholic and apostolic faith.

Memento, Domine, famulorum famularumque tuarum N et N et omnium circumstantium, quorum tibi fides cognita est, et nota devotio, pro quibus tibi offerimus: vel qui tibi offerunt hoc sacrificium laudis, pro se, suisque omnibus: pro redemptione animarum suarum, pro spe salutis, et incolumitatis suae: tibique reddunt vota sua aeterno Deo, vivo et vero.

Remember, Lord, your servants N and N. Remember all who are here about me; their faith, Lord, you have tried, their love you know. For them we do sacrifice in your honour, and they too offer it for themselves and all they love; for their souls' ransom and their safe-keeping from all harm. They now make their prayers to you, who are God eternally; the living and true God.

Memento of the Living

Special forms of the Communicantes are proper to the Feasts of Christmas, the Epiphany, Easter, the Ascension and Pentecost.

Communicantes, et memoriam venerantes, in primis gloriosae semper Virginis Mariae, Genitricis Dei et Domini nostri Jesu Christi: sed et beati Joseph, ejusdem Virginis Sponsi, et beatorum Apostolorum ac Martyrum tuorum, Petri et Pauli, Andreae, Jacobi, Joannis, Thomae, Jacobi, Philippi, Bartholomaei, Matthaei, Simonis et Thaddaei: Lini, Cleti, Clementis, Xysti, Cornelii, Cypriani, Laurentii, Chrysogoni, Joannis et Pauli, Cosmae et Damiani: et omnium Sanctorum

Here we meet in fellowship; here keep we the memory of her, first of all, the glorious ever-virgin Mary, Mother of our Lord and God, Jesus Christ. But of others, too, Joseph, the husband of the Blessed Virgin and your holy apostles and martyrs: Peter and Paul, Andrew, James, John, Thomas, James, Philip, Bartholomew, Matthew, Simon, and Jude; Linus, Cletus, Clement, Sixtus, Cornelius, Cyprian, Laurence, Chrysogonus, John and Paul, Cosmas and Damian, and all your saints everywhere. Let their merits, Lord, their intercession avail with you; shield us with your protection in every

The Invocation of the Saints

52

encounter. Through the same Christ our Lord. Amen.

tuorum; quorum meritis, precibusque concedas, ut in omnibus protectionis tuae muniamur auxilio. Per eundem Christum Dominum nostrum. Amen.

Extending his hands over the offerings, the celebrant says:

Here, then, is the offering we make to you, we who are your ministers, yet in truth it is the offering of all your household. We beseech you, Lord, to grant it favourable acceptance, ordering our days in the peace you bestow, from eternal loss delivering us, and in the company of your elect bidding our names be numbered. Through Christ our Lord. Amen.

Hanc igitur oblationem servitutis nostrae, sed et cunctae familiae tuae, quaesumus, Domine, ut placatus accipias: diesque nostros in tua pace disponas, atque ab aeterna damnatione nos eripi, et in electorum tuorum jubeas grege numerari. Per Christum Dominum nostrum. Amen.

An offering blessed and dedicated, a sacrifice truly done, worthy of our human dignity and your divine acceptance: this, O God, do you make of it, body and blood that shall be, for our sakes, of your own well-beloved Son, our Lord Jesus Christ.

Quam oblationem tu, Deus, in omnibus, quaesumus, ✠ benedictam, adscrip ✠tam, ✠ratam, rationabilem, acceptabilemque facere digneris: ut nobis ✠ Corpus, et ✠ Sanguis fiat dilectissimi Filii tui Domini nostri Jesu Christi.

He, on the eve of his Passion, took bread in those holy, those worshipful hands; to you his Father, God omnipotent, lifted his eyes heavenward, to you gave thanks, then blessed and broke and gave it to his disciples, saying:

Qui pridie quam pateretur, accepit panem in sanctas ac venerabiles manus suas, et elevatis oculis in caelum ad te Deum Patrem suum omnipotentem, tibi gratias agens, benedixit, ✠ fregit, deditque discipulis suis, dicens:

Take and eat this, all of you:

Accipite, et manducate ex hoc omnes:

With bowed head, the celebrant pronounces the words of Consecration over the bread.

Hoc est enim Corpus meum.

For this is my Body.

Having genuflected in adoration, the celebrant elevates the Sacred Host,
and then genuflects again.

Simili modo postquam coenatum est, accipiens et hunc praeclarum Calicem in sanctas ac venerabiles manus suas: item tibi gratias agens, benedixit, ✠ deditque discipulis suis, dicens:
Accipite, et bibite ex eo omnes:

So too, when supper was done, into his holy and worshipful hands he took this cup all the world holds in honour; once more he gave thanks to you, blessed and gave it to his disciples, saying:
Take and drink of this, all of you:

Bowed, the celebrant pronounces the words of Consecration over the chalice:

Hic est enim Calix Sanguinis mei, novi et aeterni testamenti: Mysterium Fidei: qui pro vobis et pro multis effundetur in remissionem peccatorum.

Haec quotiescumque feceritis, in mei memoriam facietis.

For this cup is the cup of my Blood, the seal of a new and everlasting covenant:
Faith's mystery. It is to be poured out for you and for many besides, winning pardon for your sins.
Do this, whenever you drink it, for my commemoration.

Having genuflected in adoration, the celebrant elevates the Chalice, and then genuflects again.

Unde et memores, Domine, nos servi tui, sed et plebs tua sancta, ejusdem Christi Filii tui Domini nostri tam beatae passionis necnon et ab inferis resurrectionis, sed et in caelos gloriosae ascensionis: offerimus praeclarae majestati tuae de tuis donis, ac datis, hostiam ✠ puram, hostiam ✠ sanctam, ✠ hostiam immaculatam, Panem ✠ sanctum vitae aeternae et Calicem ✠ salutis perpetuae.

Unforgotten, Lord, by us your ministers, by these faithful people, how he, your Son, Christ our Lord, underwent his most blessed passion; how he rose again from the dead and ascended into heaven in glory. And still, out of the gifts you have bestowed on us, to your surpassing majesty we offer it, a victim most pure, a victim most holy, a victim without spot; bread so holy, it brings eternal life, healing drink that shall preserve us evermore. *The Anamnesis*

Supra quae propitio ac sereno vultu respicere digneris: et accepta habere, sicuti accepta habere dignatus es munera pueri tui justi Abel, et sacrificium Patriarchae nostri Abrahae: et quod tibi obtulit summus sacerdos tuus Melchisedech, sanctum sacrificium, immaculatam hostiam.

On this look down, we pray you, with an eye gracious and content; welcome it, as you did welcome the gifts of Abel, your true servant, and the sacrifice of our father Abraham, and that which your own high priest Melchisedech brought you: a sacrifice so holy, free from all spot.

At the Anamnesis

Supplices te rogamus, omnipotens Deus, jube haec perferri per manus sancti Angeli tui in sublime altare tuum, in conspectu divinae majestatis tuae: ut quotquot ex hac altaris participatione sacrosanctum Filii tui, Corpus, et Sanguinem sumpserimus, omni benedictione caelesti et gratia repleamur. Per Christum Dominum nostrum. Amen.

We humbly implore you, O God almighty, bid one of your holy angels carry up this sacrifice to your altar high in heaven. There let it plead before your divine majesty for all who shall partake of this altar on earth. As we receive the most sacred Body and Blood of your Son, may we be filled with every blessing, every grace from above. Through the same Christ our Lord. Amen.

Memento etiam, Domine, famulorum famularumque tuarum *(N et N)* qui nos praecesserunt cum signo fidei, et dormiunt in somno pacis. Ipsis, Domine, et omnibus in Christo quiescentibus, locum refrigerii, lucis et pacis, ut indulgeas, deprecamur. Per eundem Christum Dominum nostrum. Amen.

And ever, Lord, be mindful of your servants and handmaids, *N and N,* who went before us with the seal of faith upon them, and have fallen asleep now, to rest in peace. To these, Lord, and to all who lie safe in Christ's keeping, grant a dwelling-place, we pray you, where all is refreshment, and light, and repose. Through the same Christ our Lord. Amen.

Memento of the Dead

Nobis quoque peccatoribus famulis tuis, de multitudine miserationum tuarum sperantibus, partem aliquam, et societatem donare digneris, cum tuis sanctis Apostolis et Martyribus: cum Joanne, Stephano, Matthia, Barnaba, Ignatio, Alexandro, Marcellino, Petro, Felicitate, Perpetua, Agatha, Lucia, Agnete, Caecilia, Anastasia, et omnibus Sanctis tuis intra quorum nos consortium, non aestimator meriti, sed veniae, quaesumus, largitor admitte. Per Christum Dominum nostrum.

And to us, who are servants of yours, sinners who yet put their trust in the abundance of your mercy, grant some portion yet; some fellowship with your holy apostles and martyrs, John, Stephen, Matthias, Barnabas, Ignatius, Alexander, Marcellinus, Peter, Felicity, Perpetua, Agatha, Lucy, Agnes, Cecilia, Anastasia, and of all your saints. Not weighing our merits, but free pardon bestowing, enrol us, we pray you, in their company, through Christ our Lord.

Per quem haec omnia, Domine, semper bona creas, sancti ✠ ficas, vivi ✠ ficas, bene ✠ dicis, et praestas nobis.

Through whom, Lord, these gifts of yours, do you ever create, ever hallow, ever give life, ever bless, ever confer on us.

The celebrant, having made the sign of the Cross with the Host over the Chalice and slightly elevating them both, prays the Doxology:

Through him,
and together with him,
and in his name,
to you, Father Almighty,
in the bond of the Holy Spirit,
all honour and praise is given
throughout all ages! Amen.

PER ✠ IPSUM,
et cum ✠ ipso,
et in ✠ ipso,
est tibi Deo Patri ✠ omnipotenti,
in unitate Spiritus ✠ Sancti,
omnis honor et gloria,

and he concludes with the words:

Celebrant: per omnia saecula saeculorum.

ALL RESPOND: **Amen.**

TURN TO PAGE 62

The rite of Communion

In the early Church, the Lord's Prayer was taught to the catechumens only a few weeks before baptism: it is a prayer for those initiated into the Church. Our Saviour has given us a model prayer, a prayer magnificent in its perfection of style and content, in its structure and in the spirit which pervades it; a prayer which binds together all our needs and desires and presents them to the Father in the light of his divine plan. This is a precious legacy of Christ to all his followers. And so, it is only with the greatest reverence that we should presume to recite this prayer, endeavouring to prepare ourselves beforehand and to recite it devoutly, savouring each petition to the full. The Embolism—a sort of commentary on the last petition of the Lord's Prayer—follows. Sin and its consequences are the greatest evils, and so we solemnly pray to be delivered from every evil, past, present and future.

The *Commingling* is a very ancient custom, found in all the liturgies of the East and the West, but the present form bear little relationship to the primitive ceremony, which had its origins, in fact, in the early Papal Liturgy. In addition to breaking a fragment to be placed in the chalice at the Papal Mass, the Pope would break off many other fragments which were sent to the churches of the city of Rome. The *Agnus Dei* would be chanted until this had been completed. The fragment, known as a *fermentum*, was added to the chalice at the time of the Commingling at the Mass in each of the city churches. The practice sprang from the idea that the Eucharist is the sacrament of unity and peace: ideally everyone would be gathered at the Papal Mass, but since that was impractical, the Pope sent a fragment of the Sacred Host from his Mass to all his priests in outlying districts. Originally, it was this fermentum which was carried by the subdeacon of the Mass under the humeral veil. We may look upon the Commingling in our own Mass as a glorious symbol of the unity of the Church and the unity of the Holy Sacrifice, over-riding the limitations of time and place.

58

In Rome in the earliest days, the Kiss of Peace or *Pax* was given before the Offertory, in accordance with the injunction of our Lord recorded in Saint Matthew's Gospel (5: 24). By the end of the fourth century, though, it came to occupy its present position. Originally a kiss, it soon became a stylised embrace, which is how its survives today. In the ceremonies of Solemn Mass, the celebrant recites the prayer *Domine Jesu Christe, qui dixisti Apostolis tuis* whilst the deacon kneels beside him. Thereafter, both the celebrant and the deacon kiss the altar and the celebrant gives the Pax to the deacon saying "Peace be with you." The deacon passes the Pax on to the ministers and other clergy in attendance. The giving of the Pax in the More Ancient Use of the Roman Rite stresses that it is Christ's Peace—and no other—that is given. This Peace comes from the Altar after the Agnus Dei (*Dona nobis pacem*) in strict hierarchical order. In some places, the Pax may be communicated to the Faithful, or representatives of them, by means of the *Pax-brede*, a special plate ornamented with the Lamb of Peace and Reconciliation, which is kissed first by the celebrant. The Pax and the accompanying prayer are omitted in Masses for the Dead.

The celebrant says three prayers in which we are reminded of the effect that Communion is to produce in our souls: peace, sanctification and grace. The first two prayers, which were added to the Missal in the fourteenth century, recall the Anamnesis of the Canon; the celebrant with eyes fixed upon the Sacred Host, contemplates the glory of Christ as he recites these prayers.

Through our baptism, we become members of the Mystical Body of Christ, and through Christ's Eucharistic Body, this union with Christ and with one another in Christ, is cemented and made more manifest. At the Communion it is not only the union of Christ with the individual that the liturgy has in mind, but also the great Communion of Saints into which we are drawn—the building up of the Mystical Body of Christ through the Eucharist. *The Catechism of the Catholic Church* has an excellent treatment of the Church's teaching on this Communion at paragraphs 1384–1405.

As with the *Introit* and *Offertorium*, the *Communio* was added to the Mass as a musical accompaniment to the procession of the Faithful as they approached the altar to receive Holy Communion. Originally, therefore, it consisted of the singing of a psalm, before which and after every verse of which, an antiphon was sung. By the thirteenth century (but much earlier in various places), the psalm was omitted and only the antiphon was sung: thus is it printed in the missal, although it is still permitted to sing a psalm, according to the ancient practice. The text of the *Communio* is not directly concerned with the reception of Holy Communion, but reinforces the scriptural texts used earlier in the Mass.

The Postcommunion prayer is usually formulated in such a way as to place emphasis on thanksgiving for the Sacrifice of the Mass, rather than for the reception of Holy Communion. In fact, some of the very oldest of these prayers do not mention the reception of Holy Communion at all. It is noteworthy that these prayers are written in the plural: the celebrant and all those present join in giving thanks.

The Postcommunio

Our English word "dismissal" is connected with the same Latin word that is contained in the formula *Ite, Missa est.* The popular translation of this phrase "Go, the Mass is ended" is not so much inaccurate as a record of how the word *Missa* changed its meaning through liturgical use. The word for a dismissal by the eleventh century came to be used as the word for the Eucharist itself: Mass. At a Mass for the Dead, "Go, this is the dismissal" is replaced by the phrase "May they rest in peace. Amen." But when a procession or some other liturgical function immediately follows Mass, the formula is replaced by *Benedicamus Domino* ("Let us bless the Lord"). At a Solemn Mass, the deacon gives the dismissal, which is often sung to very elaborate music. The music for the dismissal almost always is the same melody as that of the *Kyrie*: providing a musical unity to the beginning and end of the Mass.

The Dismissal

Until the middle ages, the Mass concluded with the dismissal, but the prayer *Placeat tibi, sancta Trinitas* (first found in the ninth century) was recited quietly by the celebrant as he kissed the altar and proceeded back to the sacristy. It is a very simple but beautiful prayer and is a final summation of what the celebrant had intended by offering the Mass. The celebrant turns to the people to impart the Blessing: at a Pontifical Mass, a bishop sings the formula. In fact, the final blessing is derived (in part) from the old practice of the bishop bestowing his blessing upon the Faithful as he walked from the altar to the sacristy. Priest-celebrants by the eleventh century had also begun to give a blessing before leaving the altar.

The Placeat Tibi and the Blessing

The Beginning of
the Gospel of John

This Gospel reminds us of what takes place in Holy Communion: all who receive Jesus Christ, the Word made flesh, with faith and love become with him sons of God. In the original Greek, or in Latin or in English, the beginning of John's Gospel is one of the most magnificent passages of all Holy Scripture, with a great depth of meaning. Because of its unambiguous declaration of the divine nature of Christ, this passage had long been used as a tract against heresy and grew in popular devotion, even from the time of Saint Augustine. In the twelfth century, this passage came to be recited as a prayer of thanksgiving by the celebrant as he was returning to the sacristy or as he was removing his vestments at the conclusion of Mass, but, as a recognition of the devotion of the faithful to it, it was adopted as the concluding prayer of the Mass when the Roman Missal was published in 1570. As well as being a majestic thanksgiving for what has been accomplished, this Gospel is a dramatic affirmation of the unity of the sacramental and historical orders, and of the total reliance of the economy of salvation on the redemptive Incarnation. The beginning of John's Gospel is also appointed in the Roman Ritual for recitation during the Rite of the Visitation of the Sick.

The Prayers after
Low Mass

In 1884, Pope Leo XIII ordered certain prayers to be recited after Low Mass for the needs of the Church, but in 1930, Pope Pius XI decreed that these prayers should be recited for the conversion of Russia from Communism. Since in our own day we have witnessed, on the one hand, the collapse of communism in Russia, but, on the other, a great crisis in belief within our Holy Mother, the Church, it seems timely that these greatly cherished prayers be once again offered "for the needs of the Church".

At the Lord's Prayer

THE RITE OF COMMUNION

Oremus. Praeceptis salutaribus moniti,
et divina institutione formati, audemus dicere:

*[Let us pray: directed by our Saviour's command
and following divine teaching, we dare to say:]*

and, where it customary, all may pray together with the celebrant:

Pater noster
**qui es in caelis: sanctificetur nomen tuum:
adveniat regnum tuum: fiat voluntas tua,
sicut in caelo, et in terra.
Panem nostrum quotidianum da nobis hodie:
et dimitte nobis debita nostra,
sicut et nos dimittimus debitoribus nostris.
Et ne nos inducas in tentationem.
Sed libera nos a malo. Amen.**

Deliver us, O Lord, from every evil, past, present, and to come; and graciously grant peace in our days through the intercession of the blessed and glorious ever-Virgin Mary, Mother of God, and of your blessed Apostles Peter and Paul, Andrew and all the Saints: so that helped by the riches of your mercy we may ever be free from sin and secure from every disturbance, through the same Jesus Christ our Lord, your Son, who is God, living and reigning with you, in the unity of the Holy Spirit, throughout all ages.

Libera nos, quaesumus, Domine, ab omnibus malis, praeteritis, praesentibus, et futuris: et intercedente beata et gloriosa semper Virgine Dei Genitrice Maria, cum beatis Apostolis tuis Petro et Paulo, atque Andrea, et omnibus Sanctis, da propitius pacem in diebus nostris: ut ope misericordiae tuae adjuti, et a peccato simus semper liberi, et ab omni perturbatione securi. Per eundem Dominum nostrum Jesum Christum Filium tuum, qui tecum vivit et regnat in unitate Spiritus Sancti Deus,

the celebrant concludes the prayer aloud:

Celebrant: per omnia saecula saeculorum.

ALL RESPOND: **Amen.**

The celebrant, having broken the Host over the Chalice,
makes the sign of the Cross with the Particle, before placing it in the chalice:

Celebrant: ✠   Pax Domini sit semper vobiscum.

ALL RESPOND: **Et cum spiritu tuo.**

Haec commixtio et consecratio Corporis et Sanguinis Domini nostri Jesu Christi, fiat accipientibus nobis in vitam aeternam.	May this sacramental mingling of the Body and Blood of our Lord Jesus Christ, which we are about to receive, bring us eternal life. Amen.

At a sung Mass, all sing the Agnus Dei:

KNEEL

Agnus Dei, qui tollis peccata mundi, miserere nobis. Agnus Dei, qui tollis peccata mundi, miserere nobis. Agnus Dei, qui tollis peccata mundi: dona nobis pacem.	Lamb of God, who takes away the sins of the world, have mercy on us. Lamb of God, who takes away the sins of the world, have mercy on us. Lamb of God, who takes away the sins of the world, grant us peace.

Then the celebrant makes his private preparation for Holy Communion:

Domine Jesu Christe, qui dixisti Apostolis tuis: Pacem relinquo vobis, pacem meam do vobis: ne respicias peccata mea, sed fidem Ecclesiae tuae; eamque secundum voluntatem tuam pacificare et coadunare digneris: Qui vivis et regnas Deus per omnia saecula saeculorum. Amen.	Lord Jesus Christ, who said to your Apostles, peace I leave with you, my peace I give to you; look not upon my sins but upon the faith of your Church, and be pleased to give her peace and unity according to your will. You who are God living and reigning throughout all ages. Amen.

In a Solemn Mass, the celebrant gives the Pax to the deacon.

Domine Jesu Christe, Fili Dei vivi qui ex voluntate Patris, cooperante Spiritu Sancto, per mortem tuam mundum vivificasti: libera me per hoc sacrosanctum Corpus et Sanguinem tuum ab omnibus iniquitatibus meis, et universis malis: et fac me tuis semper inhaerere mandatis, et a te numquam separari permittas: Qui cum eodem Deo Patre, et Spiritu Sancto vivis et regnas Deus in saecula saeculorum. Amen.	Lord Jesus Christ, Son of the living God, you have brought life to the world by your death, in fulfillment of the Father's will, and in a common work with the Holy Spirit. By this your most holy Body and Blood, deliver me from all my sins and from every evil. Make me always cling to your commandments and let me never be separated from you, who, with the same God the Father and the Holy Spirit, are God, living and reigning throughout all ages. Amen.

At the Ecce Agnus Dei

Perceptio Corporis tui, Domine Jesu Christe, quod ego indignus sumere praesumo, non mihi proveniat in judicium et condemnationem: sed pro tua pietate prosit mihi ad tutamentum mentis et corporis, et ad medelam percipiendam. Qui vivis et regnas cum Deo Patre in unitate Spiritus Sancti Deus, per omnia saecula saeculorum. Amen.

Let the reception of your Body, Lord Jesus Christ, which I, though unworthy, dare to receive, not result in my judgement and condemnation; but, through your kindness, let it be a safeguard and a healing remedy for my soul and body: you who, with God the Father in the unity of the Holy Spirit, are one God living and reigning throughout all ages. Amen.

Panem caelestem accipiam, et nomen Domini invocabo.

I shall take the Bread of heaven and I shall call upon the name of the Lord.

Domine, non sum dignus, ut intres sub tectum meum: sed tantum dic verbo, et sanabitur anima mea.
(three times)

Lord I am not worthy, that you should enter under my roof; say but the word and my soul shall be healed.

The celebrant reverently consumes the Body of Christ, saying:

Corpus Domini nostri Jesu Christi custodiat animam meam in vitam aeternam. Amen.

May the Body of our Lord Jesus Christ guard my soul unto eternal life. Amen.

Quid retribuam Domino pro omnibus quae retribuit mihi? Calicem salutaris accipiam, et nomen Domini invocabo. Laudans invocabo Dominum, et ab inimicis meis salvus ero.

What shall I give back to the Lord for everything which he has given to me? I shall take the Chalice of salvation and call upon the name of the Lord. I shall praise the Lord as I call upon him, and I shall be safe from my enemies.

The celebrant reverently consumes the Blood of Christ, saying:

Sanguis Domini nostri Jesu Christi custodiat animam meam in vitam aeternam. Amen.

May the Blood of our Lord Jesus Christ guard my soul unto eternal life. Amen.

The celebrant takes a host from the ciborium, turns towards the people and says:

Ecce Agnus Dei, ecce qui tollit peccata mundi:
(Behold the Lamb of God, behold him who takes away the sins of the world:)

And all say together with the celebrant three times:

Domine, non sum dignus, ut intres sub tectum meum: sed tantum dic verbo, et sanabitur anima mea.

The Faithful approach the altar to receive Holy Communion;
those receiving Holy Communion kneel (if possible) at the Communion rail
and receive the Sacred Host ON THE TONGUE.

The celebrant, making the sign of the Cross with the Particle,
distributes Holy Communion to each person saying:

**Corpus Domini nostri Jesu Christi
custodiat animam tuam in vitam aeternam. Amen.**

(May the Body of our Lord Jesus Christ guard your soul unto eternal life. Amen.)

When Holy Communion has been distributed,
the celebrant purifies the sacred vessels whilst saying:

May we receive with a pure mind, Lord, what we have received by our mouth, and may the gift we receive in this life be for us an eternal remedy.

Quod ore sumpsimus, Domine, pura mente capiamus et de munere temporali fiat nobis remedium sempiternum.

May your Body, O Lord, which I have eaten, and your Blood which I have drunk, adhere to every fibre of my being; and grant that nothing of sin's defilement may remain in me, since I am now renewed by this pure and holy sacrament; you who live and reign throughout all ages. Amen.

Corpus tuum, Domine, quod sumpsi, et Sanguis, quem potavi, adhaereat visceribus meis et praesta; ut in me non remaneat scelerum macula, quem pura et sancta refecerunt sacramenta: Qui vivis et regnas in saecula saeculorum. Amen.

THE COMMUNIO AND POSTCOMMUNIO

At a Sung Mass, the choir chants the Communio during the distribution of Holy Communion.

Having read the Communio, the celebrant greets the people:

STAND

Celebrant:	Dominus vobiscum.
ALL RESPOND:	**Et cum spiritu tuo.**
Celebrant:	Oremus.

(THE PROPER OF THE MASS FOR THE DAY)

The celebrant reads the Postcommunio, which concludes with the words:

Celebrant:	per omnia saecula saeculorum.
ALL RESPOND:	**Amen.**

THE DISMISSAL AND BLESSING

Then the celebrant greets the people again:

Celebrant: Dominus vobiscum.

ALL RESPOND: **Et cum spiritu tuo.**

Then he (or, at a Solemn Mass, the deacon) gives the dismissal:

Ite, Missa est.

ALL RESPOND: **Deo gratias.**

But at a Mass for the Dead is said:

Requiescant in pace.

ALL RESPOND: **Amen.**

Then the celebrant bows before the altar and says: **KNEEL**

Placeat tibi, sancta Trinitas, obsequium servitutis meae et praesta; ut sacrificium, quod oculis tuae majestatis indignus obtuli, tibi sit acceptabile, mihique, et omnibus, pro quibus illud obtuli, sit, te miserante, propitiabile. Per Christum Dominum nostrum. Amen.

May the tribute of my service, O holy Trinity, be pleasing to you; and grant that the sacrifice which I, though unworthy, have offered in the sight of your majesty, may be acceptable to you and, through your mercy, may it atone for my sins and for the sins of all for whom I have offered it. Through Christ our Lord. Amen.

Turning towards the people, the celebrant gives the blessing:

Benedicat vos omnipotens Deus,

✠   Pater, et Filius, et Spiritus Sanctus.

ALL RESPOND: **Amen.**

At the Last Gospel

THE BEGINNING OF THE GOSPEL OF JOHN

C. Dominus vobiscum.

Minister only: Et cum spiritu tuo.

C. ✠Initium sancti Evangelii
secundum Joannem.

M. Gloria tibi, Domine.

C. The Lord be with you.

M. And with your spirit.

C. The beginning of the holy Gospel according to John.

M. Glory to you, O Lord.

In principio erat Verbum, et Verbum erat apud Deum, et Deus erat Verbum. Hoc erat in principio apud Deum. Omnia per ipsum facta sunt et sine ipso factum est nihil, quod factum est: in ipso vita erat, et vita erat lux hominum: et lux in tenebris lucet, et tenebrae eam non comprehenderunt. Fuit homo missus a Deo, cui nomen erat Joannes. Hic venit in testimonium, ut testimonium perhiberet de lumine, ut omnes crederent per illum. Non erat ille lux, sed ut testimonium perhiberet de lumine. Erat lux vera, quae illuminat omnem hominem venientem in hunc mundum. In mundo erat, et mundus per ipsum factus est, et mundus eum non cognovit. In propria venit, et sui eum non receperunt. Quotquot autem receperunt eum, dedit eis potestatem filios Dei fieri, his, qui credunt in nomine ejus: qui non ex sanguinibus, neque ex voluntate carnis, neque ex voluntate viri, sed ex Deo nati sunt.

At the beginning of time, the Word already was, and that Word was with God: the Word was God. He was in the beginning with God. All things were made through him, and nothing that came into being, was made without him. In him was life, and that life was the light of men; the light shines in the darkness, and the darkness has not overcome it. A man appeared, sent from God, whose name was John. He came as a witness, to give testimony to the light, that all might believe through him. He was not the light, but was to bear witness to the light. The Word is the true light, who enlightens every soul born into the world. He through whom the world was made came into the world; but the world did not recognise him. He came to his own, and his own did not receive him. But to all who did receive him and who believed in his name, to these he gave power to become children of God: those who were born, not of blood, nor by the will of flesh, nor by the will of man, but are born of God.

All genuflect during the following words

Et Verbum caro factum est, et habitavit in nobis: et vidimus gloriam ejus, gloriam quasi Unigeniti a Patre, plenum gratiae et veritatis.

Minister only: Deo gratias.

And the Word was made flesh, and dwelt among us; And we saw his glory, the glory of the Only-begotten Son of the Father, full of grace and truth.

Prayers after Low Mass

KNEEL

Hail Mary, full of Grace, the Lord is with thee.
Blessed art thou among women,
and blessed is the fruit of thy womb, Jesus.

Holy Mary, Mother of God.
Pray for us sinners,
Now, and at the hour of our death. Amen.

(Hail Mary repeated three times)

Hail, holy Queen, Mother of mercy,
our life, our sweetness, and our hope!
To thee do we cry, poor banished children of Eve.
To thee do we send up our sighs, mourning and weeping in this vale of tears.
Turn then, most gracious advocate, thine eyes of mercy towards us.
And after this, our exile, show unto us the blessed fruit of thy womb, Jesus.
O clement, O loving, O sweet Virgin Mary.

Pray for us, O Holy Mother of God.
That we may be made worthy of the promises of Christ.

Let us pray.

O God, our refuge and our strength, mercifully look down upon thy people who cry to thee; and through the intercession of the glorious and immaculate Virgin Mary, Mother of God, of St. Joseph, her spouse, of thy blessed Apostles, Peter and Paul, and of all the Saints, in thy mercy and goodness hear our prayers for the conversion of sinners, and for the liberty and exaltation of our Holy Mother the Church. Through the same Christ our Lord. Amen.

All pray together:

Blessed Michael the Archangel, defend us in the hour of conflict;
be our safeguard against the wickedness and snares of the devil,
may God restrain him we humbly pray.
And do thou, O Prince of the heavenly Host,
by the power of God, thrust Satan down to hell,
and with him the other wicked spirits
who wander through the world for the ruin of souls. Amen.

Most sacred heart of Jesus, **have mercy on us.**

(three times)

Prayers of Thanksgiving after Mass

After Holy Communion
(Sarum Missal)

I pray you, O Lord, that this Holy Communion may be my guide and my food for the voyage of this life even to the harbour of my eternal salvation. Let it be my comfort when my thoughts are perplexed, a means of loving delight in all good works, patience in trial and distress, and a remedy in sickness. Grant to me, through my receiving of these sacred mysteries, a right faith, firm hope, and perfect love, courage to renounce the world, a refinement of my desires, an inward joy, a fervent loyalty to you, a remembrance and tender sympathy for the sufferings of your beloved Son, and grace to fill my life with goodness by my worship of you and the sincerity of my faith. Amen.

Sanctus, sanctus, sanctus
(Layfolk's Mass Book, 14th century)

In world of worlds without ending, thanked be thou, Jesu, my King. All my heart I give it thee, great right it is that so it be. With all my will I worship thee: blessed, Jesu, might thou be. With all my heart I thank thee the good that thou hast done to me. Sweet Jesu, grant me now this, that I may come unto thy bliss, there with angels for to sing the sweet song of thy praising: Sanctus, sanctus, sanctus. Jesus grant it be thus. Amen.

From the Pontifical of Magdalen
(11th century)

Most High God, our helper and our protector, give us, we pray you, kindly hearing and grant your mercy to us who seek it, that all who, within the walls of this church, make supplication to you, may win pardon of their sins and deserve eternal joys. Amen.

From the Benedictional of John Longdale
(16th century)

May our Lord, the Father of all mercies, sustain us by his own strength and keep alive our spirit of charity in every situation. May he give us the desire of that most valuable gift: a wide-hearted sympathy and a broad-shouldered endurance. Then shall we have experience of that wisdom which is part of the liberty of the children of God. Amen.

A prayer of the twelfth century
(Anonymous)

O my soul, the King of angels is come to make his dwelling with us. Let our hearts be wholly gladdened in the presence of so noble a guest, and let us give all honour and glory that he should so condescend to visit his servants. Joyfully let us feast with him in all happiness and delight, rejoicing in him and in all that he is. Let us render him every possible duty of loving charity, praying and beseeching him to stay with us. And if it be that we cannot do all this as perfectly as we would, at least let us be humble before him and vow ourselves to do his will. Amen.

From the Mozarabic Psalter
(11th century)

O Lord, make it one of our gifts that your teachings be ever ready in our minds. So will our way of life be a showing-forth of you and our conversation an enlightenment to those about us. So we shall live in harmony of mind with all and gain the reward of eternal life. Amen.

A prayer at departing
(Syrian Rite)

Remain in peace O divine and holy altar of the Lord, I know not if I shall return to you again or no. Grant to me, O Lord, that I may see you one day in the heavenly company of those who have gone before me, and of this I have firm hope. Remain in peace, holy altar of reparation; may your redeeming Body and Blood, which I have received therefrom, be satisfaction for my sins and forgiveness of all my failings, as also my sure trust before the throne of my Lord God forever. Remain in peace, O holy altar and table of life, to plead mercy for me from our Lord Jesus Christ, of whom may I never cease to think from this time forward and always. Amen.

A prayer to the Blessed Virgin Mary
(Saint Peter Canisius)

I salute you, glorious Mother of God, my special patron. To your motherly care I commend myself this day, that whatever is to be done during it to the glory of your Son, whether it be for my own well-being or for the good of neighbour, may all be rightly begun and fittingly ended. Help us and those who are our friends in every trial and difficulty. Amen.

SELECT PREFACES
From the 1970 Roman Missal

Amongst various decisions of the Ecclesia Dei Commission is a permission to include Prefaces from the 1970 Missale Romanum in the celebration of the 1962 Missale Romanum. A selection has been made from the 1969 Missale Romanum for this Mass-book. Those Prefaces are:

Preface of the Baptism of the Lord
Preface of the Annunciation
Preface of Pentecost
Preface of the Transfiguration
Preface of the Assumption
Preface of the Immaculate Conception
Preface of the Apostles Peter and Paul

Preface of Saint John the Baptist
Preface of the Angels
Preface of Pastors
Preface of Martyrs
Preface of Religious and Holy Virgins
Preface of Matrimony

Preface of the Baptism of the Lord

Vere dignum et justum est, aequum et salutare, nos tibi semper et ubique gratias agere: Domine, sancte Pater, omnipotens aeterne Deus: Qui miris signasti mysteriis novum in Jordane lavacrum, ut per vocem tuum inter homines crederetur; et, per Spiritum in columbae specie descendentem, Christus Servus tuus oleo perungi laetitiae ac mitti ad evangelizandum pauperibus nosceretur. Et ideo cum caelorum Virtutibus in terris te jugiter celebramus, majestatis tuae sine fine clamantes:

It is truly right and just, fitting, and helpful to our salvation, that we should at all times and in all places give thanks to you, O Lord, holy Father, almighty, everlasting God: Who wondrously revealed at the Jordan a new baptism, and through your Voice that came from heaven, manifested the dwelling of your beloved Son among men; and, through the descent of the Spirit upon him in the form of a dove, you have made him known as your Servant, anointed with the oil of gladness, and sent to preach good tidings to the poor. And therefore with all the powers of heaven we on earth continually do sing the glory of your majesty, evermore praising you and saying:

Turn to p. 51

Preface of the Annunciation

Vere dignum et justum est, aequum et salutare, nos tibi semper et ubique gratias agere: Domine, sancte Pater, omnipotens aeterne Deus: per Christum Dominum nostrum. Quem inter homines et propter homines nasciturum, Spiritus Sancti obumbrante virtute, a caelesti nuntio Virgo fidenter

It is truly right and just, fitting, and helpful to our salvation, that we should at all times and in all places give thanks to you, O Lord, holy Father, almighty, everlasting God, through Jesus Christ our Lord: Whom the Virgin heard in faithfulness, when the

73

heavenly messenger made known his coming birth among us, for our sake; and whom, overshadowed by the Holy Spirit, she carried lovingly in her chaste womb, that the truth of the promises given to the children of Israel might be fulfilled, and the hope of all peoples might wondrously be accomplished. Through whom the hosts of angels, rejoicing for eternity in your presence, do worship your majesty; with whose voices, we humbly pray, grant that ours also may be joined, that we may share their joy, evermore praising you and saying: Turn to p. 51

audivit et immaculatis visceribus amanter portavit, ut et promissiones filiis Israel perficeret veritas, et gentium exspectatio pateret ineffabiliter adimplenda. Per quem majestatem tuam adorat exercitus Angelorum, ante conspectum tuum in aeternitate laetantium. Cum quibus et nostras voces ut admitti jubeas, deprecamur, socia exsultatione, dicentes:

Preface of Pentecost

It is truly right and just, fitting, and helpful to our salvation, that we should at all times and in all places give thanks to you, O Lord, holy Father, almighty, everlasting God: For you, fulfilling the paschal mystery, have granted to us, through the fellowship of your Only-Begotten, to be your adopted children, and have this day bestowed upon us the Holy Spirit; who, through the foundation of the Church, has both endowed all nations with the knowledge of the one true God, and united the diversity of human tongues in the confession of the one faith. Therefore all earthly creation rejoices with songs of paschal gladness, while the heavenly hosts and angelic powers sing to your glory, evermore praising you and saying: Turn to p. 51

Vere dignum et justum est, aequum et salutare, nos tibi semper et ubique gratias agere: Domine, sancte Pater, omnipotens aeterne Deus. Tu enim, sacramentum paschale consummans, quibus, per Unigeniti tui consortium, filios adoptionis esse tribuisti, hodie Spiritum Sanctum es largitus; qui, principio nascentis Ecclesiae, et cunctis gentibus scientiam indidit deitatis, et linguarum diversitatem in unius fidei confessione sociavit. Quapropter, profusis paschalibus gaudiis, totus in orbe terrarum mundus exsultat. Sed et supernae virtutes atque angelicae potestates hymnum gloriae tuae concinunt, sine fine dicentes:

Preface of the Transfiguration

It is truly right and just, fitting, and helpful to our salvation, that we should at all times and in all places give thanks to you, O Lord, holy Father, almighty, everlasting God, through Jesus Christ our Lord. Who revealed his glory in the presence of chosen witnesses, when the human form he shared with them

Vere dignum et justum est, aequum et salutare, nos tibi semper et ubique gratias agere: Domine, sancte Pater, omnipotens aeterne Deus: per Christum Dominum nostrum. Qui coram electis testibus suam gloriam revelavit, et communem illam cum ceteris corporis formam maximo splendore perfudit, ut de cordibus discipulorum cruces scandalum tolleretur, et in totius Ecclesiae corpore declararet implendum quod ejus mirabiliter praefulsit in capite. Et ideo cum caelorum virtutibus in terris te jugiter celebramus, majestati tuae sine fine clamantes:

was bathed in dazzling splendour, that he might remove the shame of the cross from the hearts of the disciples, and manifest the fulfilment in the whole Church, his body, of that which marvellously shone forth in him, the same Jesus Christ her head. And therefore with all the powers of heaven we on earth continually do sing the glory of your majesty, evermore praising you and saying: Turn to p. 51

Preface of the Assumption

Vere dignum et justum est, aequum et salutare, nos tibi semper et ubique gratias agere: Domine, sancte Pater, omnipotens aeterne Deus: per Christum Dominum nostrum. Quoniam in caelos hodie Virgo Deipara est assumpta, Ecclesiae tuae consummandae initium et imago, ac populo peregrinati certae spei et solacii documentum; corruptionem enim sepulcri eam videre merito noluisti, quae Filium tuum, vitae omnis auctorem, ineffabiliter de se genuit incarnatum. Et ideo, choris angelicis sociati, te laudamus, in gaudio confitentes:

It is truly right and just, fitting, and helpful to our salvation, that we should at all times and in all places give thanks to you, O Lord, holy Father, almighty, everlasting God, through Jesus Christ our Lord. For the Virgin Mother of God was this day taken up into heaven, the beginning and sign of the consummation of your Church and to be a testimony to sure hope and comfort to your pilgrim people; for it was not your will that she should see corruption of the grave who wondrously brought forth your incarnate Son, the very author of all life. Therefore with the choirs of angels do we rejoice, evermore praising you and saying: Turn to p. 51

Preface of the Immaculate Conception

Vere dignum et justum est, aequum et salutare, nos tibi semper et ubique gratias agere: Domine, sancte Pater, omnipotens aeterne Deus: Qui beatissimam Virginem Mariam ab omni originalis culpae labe praeservasti, ut in ea, gratiae tuae plenitudine ditata, dignam Filio tuo Genetricem praepares, et Sponsae ejus Ecclesiae sine ruga vel macula formosae signares exordium. Filium enim erat purissima Virgo datura, qui crimina nostra Agnus innocens aboleret; et ipsam prae omnibus tuo populo disponebas advocatam gratiae et sanctitatis examplar. Et ideo, choris

It is truly right and just, fitting, and helpful to our salvation, that we should at all times and in all places give thanks to you, O Lord, holy Father, almighty, everlasting God: who preserved the blessed Virgin Mary from all stain of original sin, that in her, enriched by the fullness of your grace, you might prepare for your Son a fitting Mother, and foreshadow the beginning of the Church, his spouse, having neither spot nor wrinkle. For the most pure Virgin was to bring forth a Son who, the innocent Lamb, would do away our offences, and would herself be in

76

all things an advocate for your people, and a pattern of grace and sanctity. Therefore with the choirs of angels we rejoice and worship you, evermore praising you and saying:

Turn to p. 51

angelicis sociati, te laudamus, in gaudio confitentes:

Preface of the Apostles Peter and Paul

It is truly right and just, fitting, and helpful to our salvation, that we should at all times and in all places give thanks to you, O Lord, holy Father, almighty, everlasting God: who causes us to rejoice in the blessed apostles Peter and Paul. For Saint Peter you chose to be our leader to preach the faith and found the infant Church among the remnant of Israel; while Saint Paul did teach and make clear that faith, going forth to enlighten and instruct the pagan nations whom you also called into your Church. Thus by a diverse plan gathering together the one family of Christ they are given equal honour in this world and share one crown in heaven. Therefore with all the Saints and Angels we glorify your name, evermore praising you and saying:

Turn to p. 51

Vere dignum et justum est, aequum et salutare, nos tibi semper et ubique gratias agere: Domine, sancte Pater, omnipotens aeterne Deus: Quia nos beati apostoli Petrus et Paulus tua dispositione laetificant: hic princeps fidei confitendae, ille intelligendae clarus assertor; hic reliquiis Israel instituens Ecclesiam primitivam, ille magister et doctor gentium vocandarum. Sic diverso consilio unam Christi familiam congregantes, par mundo venerabile, una corona sociavit. Et ideo cum Sanctis et Angelis universes te collaudames, sine fine dicentes:

Preface of John the Baptist

It is truly right and just, fitting, and helpful to our salvation, that we should at all times and in all places give thanks to you, O Lord, holy Father, almighty, everlasting God, through Jesus Christ our Lord: In whose forerunner Saint John we praise your wondrous works, who set him apart especially amongst those born of women. For he who by his birth had been the cause of great rejoicing, although not yet born, leapt for joy at the coming of our salvation; who alone among all the prophets made known the Lamb of our redemption; who also did baptise the author of our baptism in the streams of water which were thereby made holy; and at the end was

Vere dignum et justum est, aequum et salutare, nos tibi semper et ubique gratias agere: Domine, sancte Pater, omnipotens aeterne Deus: per Christum Dominum nostrum. In cujus Praecursore beato Joanne tuam magnificentiam collaudamus, quem inter natos mulierem honore praecipuo consecrasti. Qui cum nascendo multa gaudia praestitisset, et nondum editus exsultasset ad humanae salutis adventum, ipse solus omnium prophetarum Agnum redemptionem ostendit. Sed et sanctificandis etiam aquae fluentis ipsum baptismatis lavit auctorem, et meruit fuso sanguine supremum illi testimonium exhibere. Et ideo, cum caelorum Virtutibus, in terris te jugiter praedicamus, majestati tuae sine fine clamantes:

found worthy by the shedding of his blood to bear witness unto him. Therefore with all the powers of heaven, we on earth continually do glorify your majesty, evermore praising you and saying: Turn to p. 51

Preface of the Angels

Vere dignum et justum est, aequum et salutare, nos tibi semper et ubique gratias agere: Domine, sancte Pater, omnipotens aeterne Deus: Et in Archangelis Angelisque tuis tua praeconia non tacere, quia ad excellentiam tuam recurrit et gloriam quod angelica creatura tibi probabilis honoretur: et, cum illa sit amplo decore dignissima, tu quam sis immensus et super omnia praeferendus ostenderis, per Christum Dominum nostrum. Per quem multitudo Angelorum tuam celebrat majestatem, quibus adorantes in exsultatione conjungimur, una cum eis laudis voce clamantes:

It is truly right and just, fitting, and helpful to our salvation, that we should at all times and in all places give thanks to you, O Lord, holy Father, almighty, everlasting God. For we ought not be silent in praising you for your archangels and angels because when your angelic creation is fittingly honoured it reflects your surpassing glory; and whilst you constituted them in a wonderful order, you reveal yourself as measureless and above all things, through Jesus Christ our Lord. Through whom the multitude of angels do praise your majesty, with whom we unite ourselves in joy and adoration, evermore praising you and saying: Turn to p. 51

Preface of Pastors

Vere dignum et justum est, aequum et salutare, nos tibi semper et ubique gratias agere: Domine, sancte Pater, omnipotens aeterne Deus: per Christum Dominum nostrum. Quia sic tribuis Ecclesiam tuam sancti N Festivate gaudere, ut eam exemplo piae conversationis corrobores, verbo praedicationis erudias, grataque tibi supplicatione tuearis. Et ideo, cum Angelorum atque Sanctorum turba, hymnum laudis tibi canimus, sine fine dicentes:

It is truly right and just, fitting, and helpful to our salvation, that we should at all times and in all places give thanks to you, O Lord, holy Father, almighty, everlasting God, through Jesus Christ our Lord: For you have granted to your Church so to rejoice on the feast of Saint N that it may be strengthened by the example of his life, instructed by the words of his preaching, and defended in answer to his prayers. Therefore with angels and archangels, and with all the company of heaven, we bless and glorify your holy name, evermore praising you and saying:

Turn to p. 51

Preface of Martyrs

It is truly right and just, fitting, and helpful to our salvation, that we should at all times and in all places give thanks to you, O Lord, holy Father, almighty, everlasting God: Because for the confession of your name the blessed martyr N shed his [her] own blood in imitation of Christ, manifesting that wonder wherein you bring courage out of human frailty and strengthen the weak to bear witness to you, through Jesus Christ our Lord. Therefore with angels and archangels, and with all the company of heaven, we bless and glorify your holy name, evermore praising you and saying: Turn to p. 51

Vere dignum et justum est, aequum et salutare, nos tibi semper et ubique gratias agere: Domine, sancte Pater, omnipotens aeterne Deus. Quoniam beati martyris N pro confessione nominis tui, ad imitationem Christi, sanguis effusus tua mirabilia manifestat, quibus perficis in fragilitate virtutem, et vires infirmas ad testimonium roboras, per Christum Dominum nostrum. Et ideo, cum caelorum Virtutibus, in terris te jugiter celebramus, majestati tuae sine fine clamantes:

Preface of Religious and Holy Virgins

It is truly right and just, fitting, and helpful to our salvation, that we should at all times and in all places give thanks to you, O Lord, holy Father, almighty, everlasting God: And that for the saints who, for the sake of the kingdom of heaven, have dedicated themselves to Christ, it is fitting that we should honour your wondrous providence, by which you restore human nature to that state of holiness into which it was first created, and bring us to enjoy the gifts of the world to come. Therefore with angels and archangels, and with all the company of heaven, we bless and glorify your holy name, evermore praising you and saying: Turn to p. 51

Vere dignum et justum est, aequum et salutare, nos tibi semper et ubique gratias agere: Domine, sancte Pater, omnipotens aeterne Deus: In Sanctis enim, qui Christo se dedicaverunt propter regnum caelorum, tuam decet providentiam celebrare mirabilem, qua humanam substantiam et ad primae originis revocas sanctitatem, et ad experienda dona, quae in novo saeculo sunt habenda, perducis. Et ideo, cum Sanctis et Angelis universis, te collaudamus, sine fine dicentes:

Preface of Matrimony

Vere dignum et justum est, aequum et salutare, nos tibi semper et ubique gratias agere: Domine, sancte Pater, omnipotens aeterne Deus per Christum Dominum nostrum: Qui foedera nuptiarum blando concordiae jugo et insolubili pacis vinculo nexuisti, ut multiplicandis adoptionum filiis sanctorum connubiorum fecunditas pudica serviret. Tua enim, Domine, providentia, tuaque gratia ineffabilibus modis utrumque dispensas, ut, quod generatio ad mundi produxit ornatum, regeneratio ad Ecclesiae perducat augmentum: per Christum Dominum nostrum. Per quem, cum Angelis et omnibus Sanctis, hymnum laudis tibi canimus, sine fine dicentes:

It is truly right and just, fitting, and helpful to our salvation, that we should at all times and in all places give thanks to you, O Lord, holy Father, almighty, everlasting God, through Jesus Christ our Lord: Because you have enjoined a new covenant with your people so that those whom you have redeemed by Christ's death and resurrection you cause to be a part of the divine life in him and heirs to his glory in heaven. In this covenant, a holy plenitude of your grace, you have symbolised the marriage covenant which is between man and woman so that the mystery of your love, which passes all understanding may be recalled when this sacrament is celebrated among us. Therefore with angels and archangels, and with all the company of heaven, we bless and glorify your holy name, evermore praising you and saying:

Turn to p. 51

APOSTOLIC LETTER
Summorum Pontificum
of the Supreme Pontiff Benedict XVI

given motu proprio.

It has been the constant concern of the Supreme Pontiffs, and up to the present time, to ensure that the Church of Christ offers a worthy worship to the Divine Majesty, "to the praise and glory of His name," and "to the benefit of all His Holy Church."

Since time immemorial it has been necessary—as it is also for the future—to maintain the principle according to which "each particular Church must concur with the universal Church, not only as regards the doctrine of the faith and the sacramental signs, but also as regards the usages universally accepted by uninterrupted apostolic tradition, which must be observed not only to avoid errors but also to transmit the integrity of the faith, because the Church's law of prayer corresponds to her law of faith." (1)

Among the pontiffs who showed that requisite concern, particularly outstanding is the name of St. Gregory the Great, who made every effort to ensure that the new peoples of Europe received both the Catholic faith and the treasures of worship and culture that had been accumulated by the Romans in preceding centuries. He commanded that the form of the sacred liturgy as celebrated in Rome (concerning both the Sacrifice of Mass and the Divine Office) be conserved. He took great concern to ensure the dissemination of monks and nuns who, following the Rule of St. Benedict, together with the announcement of the Gospel illustrated with their lives the wise provision of their Rule that "nothing should be placed before the work of God." In this way the sacred liturgy, celebrated according to the Roman use, enriched not only the faith and piety but also the culture of many peoples. It is known, in fact, that the Latin liturgy of the Church in its various forms, in each century of the Christian era, has been a spur to the spiritual life of many saints, has reinforced many peoples in the virtue of religion and fecundated their piety.

Many other Roman pontiffs, in the course of the centuries, showed particular solicitude in ensuring that the sacred liturgy accomplished this task more effectively. Outstanding among them is St. Pius V who, sustained by great pastoral zeal and following the exhortations of the Council of Trent, renewed the entire liturgy of the Church, oversaw the publication of liturgical books amended and "renewed in accordance with the norms of the Fathers," and provided them for the use of the Latin Church.

One of the liturgical books of the Roman rite is the Roman Missal, which developed in the city of Rome and, with the passing of the centuries, little by little took forms very similar to that it has had in recent times.

"It was towards this same goal that succeeding Roman Pontiffs directed their energies during the subsequent centuries in order to ensure that the rites and liturgical books were brought up to date and when necessary clarified. From the beginning of this century they undertook a more general reform." (2) Thus our predecessors Clement VIII, Urban VIII, St. Pius X (3), Benedict XV, Pius XII and Blessed John XXIII all played a part.

In more recent times, Vatican Council II expressed a desire that the respectful reverence due to divine worship should be renewed and adapted to the needs of our time. Moved by this desire our predecessor, the Supreme Pontiff Paul VI, approved, in 1970, reformed and partly renewed liturgical books for the Latin Church. These, translated into the various languages of the world, were willingly accepted by bishops, priests and faithful. John Paul II amended the third typical edition of the Roman Missal. Thus Roman pontiffs have operated to ensure that "this kind of liturgical edifice...should again appear resplendent for its dignity and harmony." (4)

But in some regions, no small numbers of faithful adhered and continue to adhere with great love and affection to the earlier liturgical forms. These had so deeply marked their culture and their spirit that in 1984 the Supreme Pontiff John Paul II, moved by a concern for the pastoral care of these faithful, with the special indult "Quattuor abhinc anno", issued by the Congregation for Divine Worship, granted permission to use the Roman Missal published by Blessed John XXIII in the year 1962. Later, in the year 1988, John Paul II with the Apostolic Letter given as Motu Proprio, "Ecclesia Dei", exhorted bishops to make generous use of this power in favor of all the faithful who so desired.

Our predecessor John Paul II having already considered the insistent petitions of these faithful, having listened to the views of the Cardinal Fathers of the Consistory of 22 March 2006, having reflected deeply upon all aspects of the question, invoked the Holy Spirit and trusting in the help of God, with these Apostolic Letters We establish the following:

Art. 1 The Roman Missal promulgated by Paul VI is the ordinary expression of the Lex orandi (Law of prayer) of the Catholic Church of the Latin rite. Nonetheless, the Roman Missal promulgated by St. Pius V and reissued by Blessed John XXIII is to be considered as an extraordinary expression of that same Lex orandi, and must be given due honour for its venerable and ancient usage. These two expressions of the Church's Lex orandi will in no way lead to a division in the Church's Lex credendi (Law of belief). They are, in fact, two usages of the one Roman rite.

It is, therefore, permissible to celebrate the Sacrifice of the Mass following the typical edition of the Roman Missal promulgated by Blessed John XXIII in 1962 and never abrogated, as an extraordinary form of the Liturgy of the Church. The conditions for the use of this Missal as laid down by earlier documents "Quattuor abhinc annis" and "Ecclesia Dei", are substituted as follows:

Art. 2 In Masses celebrated without the people, each Catholic priest of the Latin rite, whether secular or regular, may use the Roman Missal published by Blessed Pope John XXIII in 1962, or the Roman Missal promulgated by Pope Paul VI in 1970, and may do so on any day with the exception of the Easter Triduum. For such celebrations, with either one Missal or the other, the priest has no need for permission from the Apostolic See or from his Ordinary.

Art. 3 Communities of Institutes of consecrated life and of Societies of apostolic life, of either pontifical or diocesan right, wishing to celebrate Mass in accordance with the edition of the Roman Missal promulgated in 1962, for conventual or "community" celebration in their oratories, may do so. If an individual community or an entire Institute or Society wishes to undertake such celebrations often, habitually or permanently, the decision must be taken by the Superiors Major, in accordance with the law and following their own specific decrees and statutes.

Art. 4 Celebrations of Mass as mentioned above in art. 2 may—observing all the norms of law —also be attended by faithful who, of their own free will, ask to be admitted.

Art. 5 § 1 In parishes, where there is a stable group of faithful who adhere to the earlier liturgical tradition, the pastor should willingly accept their requests to celebrate the Mass according to the rite of the Roman Missal published in 1962, and ensure that the welfare of these faithful harmonises with the ordinary pastoral care of the parish, under the guidance of the bishop in accordance with canon 392, avoiding discord and favouring the unity of the whole Church.

§ 2 Celebration in accordance with the Missal of Blessed John XXIII may take place on working days; while on Sundays and feast days one such celebration may also be held.

§ 3 For faithful and priests who request it, the pastor should also allow celebrations in this extraordinary form for special circumstances such as marriages, funerals or occasional celebrations, e.g. pilgrimages.

§ 4 Priests who use the Missal of Blessed John XXIII must be qualified to do so [in good standing] and not juridically impeded.

§ 5 In churches that are not parish or conventual churches, it is the duty of the Rector of the church to grant the above permission.

Art. 6 In Masses celebrated in the presence of the people in accordance with the Missal of Blessed John XXIII, the readings may be given in the vernacular, using editions recognised by the Apostolic See.

Art. 7 If a group of lay faithful, as mentioned in art. 5 § 1, has not obtained satisfaction to their requests from the pastor, they should inform the diocesan bishop. The bishop is strongly requested to satisfy their wishes. If he cannot arrange for such celebration to take place, the matter should be referred to the Pontifical Commission "Ecclesia Dei".

Art. 8 A bishop who, desirous of satisfying such requests, but who for various reasons is unable to do so, may refer the problem to the Commission "Ecclesia Dei" to obtain counsel and assistance.

Art. 9 § 1 The pastor, having attentively examined all aspects, may also grant permission to use the earlier ritual for the administration of the Sacraments of Baptism, Marriage, Penance, and the Anointing of the Sick, if the good of souls would seem to require it.

§ 2 Ordinaries are given the right to celebrate the Sacrament of Confirmation using the earlier Roman Pontifical, if the good of souls would seem to require it.

§ 3 Clerics ordained "in sacris constitutis" may use the Roman Breviary promulgated by Bl. John XXIII in 1962.

Art. 10 The ordinary of a particular place, if he feels it appropriate, may erect a personal parish in accordance with can. 518 for celebrations following the ancient form of the Roman rite, or appoint a chaplain, while observing all the norms of law.

Art. 11 The Pontifical Commission "Ecclesia Dei" (5) , erected by John Paul II in 1988, continues to exercise its function. Said Commission will have the form, duties and norms that the Roman Pontiff wishes to assign it.

Art. 12 This Commission, apart from the powers it enjoys, will exercise the authority of the Holy See, supervising the observance and application of these dispositions.

We order that everything We have established with these Apostolic Letters, issued as Motu Proprio, be considered as "established and decreed", and to be observed from 14th September of this year, Feast of the Exaltation of the Cross, whatever there may be to the contrary.

From Rome, at St. Peter's, 7th July 2007, third year of Our Pontificate.

Reprinted by permission of Libreria Editrice Vaticana.

1. *General Instruction of the Roman Missal*, 3rd ed., 2002, no. 397.

2. John Paul II, Apostolic Letter "Vicesimus quintus annus", 4 December 1988, 3: AAS 81 (1989), 899.

3. Ibid.

4. St. Pius X, Apostolic Letter Motu propio data, "Abhinc duos annos", 23 October 1913: AAS 5 (1913), 449-450; cf John Paul II, Apostolic Letter "Vicesimus quintus annus", no. 3: AAS 81 (1989), 899.

5. Cf. John Paul II, Apostolic Letter Motu proprio data *"Ecclesia Dei"*, 2 July 1988, 6: AAS 80 (1988), 1498.

LETTER OF HIS HOLINESS
BENEDICT XVI
to the Bishops on the Occasion of the Publication
of the Apostolic Letter "Motu Proprio Data"
Summorum Pontificum
on the Use of the Roman Liturgy
Prior to the Reform of 1970

My dear Brother Bishops,

With great trust and hope, I am consigning to you as Pastors the text of a new Apostolic Letter "Motu Proprio data" on the use of the Roman liturgy prior to the reform of 1970. The document is the fruit of much reflection, numerous consultations and prayer.

News reports and judgments made without sufficient information have created no little confusion. There have been very divergent reactions ranging from joyful acceptance to harsh opposition, about a plan whose contents were in reality unknown.

This document was most directly opposed on account of two fears, which I would like to address somewhat more closely in this letter.

In the first place, there is the fear that the document detracts from the authority of the Second Vatican Council, one of whose essential decisions—the liturgical reform—is being called into question. This fear is unfounded. In this regard, it must first be said that the Missal published by Paul VI and then republished in two subsequent editions by John Paul II, obviously is and continues to be the normal Form—the *Forma ordinaria*—of the Eucharistic Liturgy. The last version of the *Missale Romanum* prior to the Council, which was published with the authority of Pope John XXIII in 1962 and used during the Council, will now be able to be used as a *Forma extraordinaria* of the liturgical celebration. It is not appropriate to speak of these two versions of the Roman Missal as if they were "two Rites". Rather, it is a matter of a twofold use of one and the same rite.

As for the use of the 1962 Missal as a *Forma extraordinaria* of the liturgy of the Mass, I would like to draw attention to the fact that this Missal was never juridically abrogated and, consequently, in principle, was always permitted. At the time of the introduction of the new Missal, it did not seem necessary to issue specific norms for the possible use of the earlier Missal. Probably it was thought that it would be a matter of a few individual cases which would be resolved, case by case, on the local level. Afterwards, however, it soon became apparent that a good number of people remained strongly attached to this usage of the Roman Rite, which had been familiar to them from childhood. This was especially the case in countries where the liturgical movement had provided many people with a notable liturgical formation and a deep, personal familiarity with the earlier Form of the liturgical celebration. We all know that, in the movement led by Archbishop Lefebvre, fidelity to the old Missal became an external mark of identity; the reasons for the break which arose over this, however, were at a deeper level. Many people who clearly accepted the binding character of the Second Vatican Council, and were faithful to the Pope and the Bishops, nonetheless also desired to recover the form of the sacred liturgy that was dear to them. This occurred above all because in many places celebrations were not faithful to the prescriptions of the new Missal, but the latter actually was understood as authorizing or even requiring creativity, which frequently led to deformations of the liturgy which were hard to bear. I am speaking from experience, since I too lived through that period with all its hopes and its confusion. And I have seen how arbitrary deformations of the liturgy caused deep pain to individuals totally rooted in the faith of the Church.

Pope John Paul II thus felt obliged to provide, in his Motu Proprio *Ecclesia Dei* (2nd July 1988), guidelines for the use of the 1962 Missal; that document, however, did not contain detailed prescriptions but appealed in a general way to the generous response of Bishops towards the "legitimate aspirations" of those members of the faithful who requested this usage of the Roman Rite. At the time, the Pope primarily wanted to assist the Society of Saint Pius X to recover full unity with the Successor of Peter, and sought to heal a wound experienced ever more painfully. Unfortunately this reconciliation has not yet come about. Nonetheless, a number of communities have gratefully made use of the possibilities provided by the Motu Proprio. On the other hand, difficulties remain concerning the use of the 1962 Missal outside of these groups, because of the lack of precise juridical norms, particularly because Bishops, in such cases, frequently feared that the authority of the Council would be called into question. Immediately after the Second Vatican Council it was presumed that requests for the use of the 1962 Missal would be limited to the older generation which had grown up with it, but in the meantime it has clearly been demonstrated that young persons too have discovered this liturgical form, felt its attraction and found in it a form of encounter with the Mystery of the Most Holy Eucharist, particularly suited to them. Thus the need has arisen for a clearer juridical regulation which had not been foreseen at the time of the 1988 Motu Proprio. The present Norms are also meant to free Bishops from constantly having to evaluate anew how they are to respond to various situations.

In the second place, the fear was expressed in discussions about the awaited Motu Proprio, that the possibility of a wider use of the 1962 Missal would lead to disarray or even divisions within parish communities. This fear also strikes me as quite unfounded. The use of the old Missal presupposes a certain degree of liturgical formation and some knowledge of the Latin language; neither of these is found very often. Already from these concrete presuppositions, it is clearly seen that the new Missal will certainly remain the ordinary Form of the Roman Rite, not only on account of the juridical norms, but also because of the actual situation of the communities of the faithful.

It is true that there have been exaggerations and at times social aspects unduly linked to the attitude of the faithful attached to the ancient Latin liturgical tradition. Your charity and pastoral prudence will be an incentive and guide for improving these. For that matter, the two Forms of the usage of the Roman Rite can be mutually enriching: new Saints and some of the new Prefaces can and should be inserted in the old Missal. The "*Ecclesia Dei*" Commission, in contact with various bodies devoted to the *usus antiquior*, will study the practical possibilities in this regard. The celebration of the Mass according to the Missal of Paul VI will be able to demonstrate, more powerfully than has been the case hitherto, the sacrality which attracts many people to the former usage. The most sure guarantee that the Missal of Paul VI can unite parish communities and be loved by them consists in its being celebrated with great reverence in harmony with the liturgical directives. This will bring out the spiritual richness and the theological depth of this Missal.

I now come to the positive reason which motivated my decision to issue this Motu Proprio updating that of 1988. It is a matter of coming to an interior reconciliation in the heart of the Church. Looking back over the past, to the divisions which in the course of the centuries have rent the Body of Christ, one continually has the impression that, at critical moments when divisions were coming about, not enough was done by the Church's leaders to maintain or regain reconciliation and unity. One has the impression that omissions on the part of the Church have had their share of blame for the fact that these divisions were able to harden. This glance at the past imposes an obligation on us today: to make every effort to enable for all those who truly desire unity to remain in that unity or to attain it anew. I think of a sentence in the Second Letter to the Corinthians, where Paul writes: "Our mouth is open to you, Corinthians; our heart is wide. You are not restricted by us, but you are restricted in your own affections. In return... widen your hearts also!" (2 Cor 6:11–13). Paul was certainly speaking in another context, but his exhortation can and must touch us too, precisely on this subject. Let us generously open our hearts and make room for everything that the faith itself allows.

There is no contradiction between the two editions of the Roman Missal. In the history of the liturgy there is growth and progress, but no rupture. What earlier generations held as sacred, remains sacred and great for us too, and it cannot be all of a sudden entirely forbidden or even considered harmful. It behooves all of us to preserve the riches which have developed in the Church's faith and prayer, and to give them their proper place. Needless to say, in order to experience full communion, the priests of the communities adhering to the former usage cannot, as a matter of principle, exclude celebrating according to the new books. The total exclusion of the new rite would not in fact be consistent with the recognition of its value and holiness.

In conclusion, dear Brothers, I very much wish to stress that these new norms do not in any way lessen your own authority and responsibility, either for the liturgy or for the pastoral care of your faithful. Each Bishop, in fact, is the moderator of the liturgy in his own Diocese (cf. *Sacrosanctum Concilium*, 22: "Sacrae Liturgiae moderatio ab Ecclesiae auctoritate unice pendet quae quidem est apud Apostolicam Sedem et, ad normam iuris, apud Episcopum").

Nothing is taken away, then, from the authority of the Bishop, whose role remains that of being watchful that all is done in peace and serenity. Should some problem arise which the parish priest cannot resolve, the local Ordinary will always be able to intervene, in full harmony, however, with all that has been laid down by the new norms of the Motu Proprio.

Furthermore, I invite you, dear Brothers, to send to the Holy See an account of your experiences, three years after this Motu Proprio has taken effect. If truly serious difficulties come to light, ways to remedy them can be sought.

Dear Brothers, with gratitude and trust, I entrust to your hearts as Pastors these pages and the norms of the Motu Proprio. Let us always be mindful of the words of the Apostle Paul addressed to the presbyters of Ephesus: "Take heed to yourselves and to all the flock, in which the Holy Spirit has made you overseers, to care for the Church of God which he obtained with the blood of his own Son" (Acts 20:28).

I entrust these norms to the powerful intercession of Mary, Mother of the Church, and I cordially impart my Apostolic Blessing to you, dear Brothers, to the parish priests of your dioceses, and to all the priests, your co-workers, as well as to all your faithful.

Given at Saint Peter's, 7th July 2007

Commission "Ecclesia Dei"
Decisions of the Pontifical Commission concerning Celebrations of the 1962 Missale Romanum

No. 24/92 Rome, 7th June, 1993.

1.	In celebrating the Solemn High Mass according to the 1962 Roman Missal it is necessary to follow the rubrics of that Missal. In the past the employment of a person who had received the ministry of acolyte acting as subdeacon was tolerated. In that case, the acolyte acting as subdeacon did not wear the maniple. This usage may continue to be tolerated.

3.	It is permissible for those serving Mass to wear amice, alb and cincture if this is what is ordinarily worn by the servers in the parish where the Mass is celebrated.

4.	With regard to the celebration of the Masses of saints canonized since 1962, the Latin orations published in the Missal of Pope Paul VI and those subsequently published by the Congregation for Divine Worship and the Discipline of the Sacraments should be used, taking the remaining parts from the Common.

No. 40/97 Rome, 26th March, 1997.

1.	This Pontifical Commission sees no difficulty in the celebrant's reading an approved vernacular translation of the Epistle and Gospel proper to the 1962 Missal while otherwise adhering to the rubrics laid down in the *Ritus Servandus*.

2.	Concerning the celebration of Solemn Pontifical and Solemn Masses:

a)	This Pontifical Commission sees no difficulty in the celebrant and ministers joining in the singing of the plainchant Gloria and Credo together with the schola cantorum and the congregation instead of reading them privately as directed by the *Ritus Servandus*. This usage was already admitted by the Church a relatively short time after the publication of the 1962 Roman Missal. The same holds true, *mutatis mutandis* for the *Missa Cantata*.

b) This Pontifical Commission sees no difficulty in the entire congregation's singing of the *Pater Noster* in all sung Masses.

With regard to all of the above matters, this Pontifical Commission has already made similar provision for the Conventual Masses celebrated in the Benedictine abbeys in France which have been granted the use of the liturgical books in force in 1962. We...believe that it may be readily applied to parochial situations as well.

3. This Pontifical Commission sees no difficulty in the use of the Prefaces which Your Lordship indicated [i.e. those additional prefaces included in the so-called "Interim Rite" Missal of 1964: editor], since they were once permitted by indults of the Congregation of Rites. Furthermore, the very rich prefaces of the Missal of Pope Paul VI could equally be used for the appropriate Masses in the 1962 *Roman Missal*. Even though the original Indult *Quattuor Abhinc Annos* of 3rd October 1984 insisted that "there must be no interchanging of texts and rites of the two Missals", this Pontifical Commission has consistently argued in the light of the "wide and generous application of the directives already issued...for the use of the Roman Missal according to the typical edition of 1962" (*Ecclesia Dei* 6,c) such usage would be fully acceptable.

Provision for the celebration of the Sung Conventual Mass of the Benedictine Communities in France using the 1962 Liturgical Books

1. Quando Missa conventualis sequitur aliquam partem Divini Officii, incheoetur cum cantu Introitus, ommissis precibus ad initium Missae.
2. Liturgia Verbi celebretur ad sedile.
3. Lectiones proferentur versus populum, sive lingua latina sive vernacula; celebrans non repetit nec lectiones nec cantus chori aut populi.
4. Proprio loco, id est post "Oremus" ante Offertorium, adhiberi possunt Preces universales juxta formulas in libris liturgicis contentas, aut aliter rite approbatas.
5. Oratio super oblata cantetur.
6. Doxologia "Per ipsum" a sacerdote celebrante cantetur, dum ipse calicem cum hostia super altare elevat, usque ad finem doxologiae, choro respondente "Amen".
7. Pater noster ab omnibus simul cum celebrante cantetur.
8. Benedictio finalis cantetur, post quam omittitur lectio initii Evangelii secundum Joannem.

Reprinted by permission of Libreria Editrice Vaticana.